W9-BVA-755

THE LION
AND THE
HONEYCOMB

The Lion
AND THE
Honeycomb

THE RELIGIOUS WRITINGS OF

TOLSTOY

EDITED AND WITH
AN INTRODUCTION BY
A. N. WILSON

TRANSLATED BY
ROBERT CHANDLER

1817

Harper & Row, Publishers, San Francisco

Cambridge, Hagerstown, New York, Philadelphia, Washington
London, Mexico City, São Paulo, Singapore, Sydney

FIRST EDITION

Library of Congress Cataloging-in-Publication Data
Tolstoy, Leo, graf, 1828–1910.
    The lion and the honeycomb.

    Bibliography: p.
    1. Christianity. I. Wilson, A. N., 1950–
II. Title.
BR75.T65213   1987   200   87–46232
ISBN 0–06–250968–3

88 89 90 91 92 RRD 10 9 8 7 6 5 4 3 2 1

Contents

Introduction

Count Lev Nikolayevich Tolstoy lived from 1828 to 1910. A large part of the excitement of his novels is the discovery of an active moral world. Other novelists have written about the workings of conscience, but few have done so as vividly as Tolstoy. He was able to write about our awareness of right and wrong with the same naturalness as he might describe, with his incomparable photographic clarity, a battle, a ball or a storm. 'All human life, we could say, consists in just these two activities (1) bringing one's behaviour into harmony with conscience or (2) hiding from oneself the promptings of conscience so as to be able to go on living as one lived before.'[1] *War and Peace*, *Anna Karenina* and *Resurrection* all take this dictum for granted. Our moral awareness, for Tolstoy, is an inherent part of our being alive.

Side by side with this intense moral awareness in Tolstoy, there is also an almost amoral humility in the face of great creating nature. It is a strain which we might associate more with the wisdom of the East than with that of the West. One thinks of Prince Andrew, wounded at Austerlitz. 'How was it I did not see that lofty sky before? And how happy I am to have found it at last! Yes! All is Vanity!, all is falsehood, except that infinite sky. There is nothing, nothing but that. But even it does not exist, there is nothing but quiet and peace. Thank God!'[2] We find this strain of oriental detachment in all Tolstoy's works, at the beginning of his life as at the end. There is a strange kinship between the Falstaffian rascal 'Uncle' Yeroshka in *Cossacks* and the nameless old man on the ferryboat in *Resurrection*. Though one is a womanizer and a swindler, and the other is some kind of holy idiot, both are in tune with the nature of things, in the way that more westernized, cerebral characters are not.

Tolstoy did not feel in tune with things – though he yearned to.

In background, from a large aristocratic land-owning family, he was a strange mixture of the earthy peasant culture of rural Russia (glimpsed and romanticized in the country estate of Yasnaya Polyana, where he grew up, and lived all his life) and of a pure European man of the Enlightenment. As a child, he had been fascinated by the wandering pilgrims and holy men who tramped up and down the road by his house, and who, encouraged by a pious aunt, came into the conservatory to eat bread and soup or to pray. At the same time, he had read Rousseau, Voltaire, Proudhon, and was, in the simple sense of the word, a rationalist. Even in his 'religious' maturity, we find him, in his diary, chuckling over Voltaire.

All these strains in Tolstoy's background and make-up must be borne in mind when we consider his specifically religious writings. We cannot change who we are. To under er-natural experience of conversion is not to abandon all that made up the natural unregenerate man.

At an early age, when he was a young soldier in the Crimean War, Tolstoy had dreamed of founding a purely ethical religion.

> Yesterday a conversation about divinity and faith inspired me with a great idea, a stupendous idea, to the realization of which I feel capable of devoting my life. This idea is the founding of a new religion appropriate to the stage of development of mankind – the religion of Christ, but purged of beliefs and mysticism, a practical religion, not promising future bliss but giving bliss on earth. . . .[3]

As readers of Tolstoy's biography will know, he did not settle down to achieving this aim as soon as he had thought of it. He left the army at the age of twenty-six, travelled, went into 'society', experimented with various liberal reforms on his estates, and took an interest in educating the children of his peasants. He married, in the autumn of 1862, the highly-strung daughter of a court doctor in Moscow, and they were to have thirteen children. And in addition, he wrote a series of novels and stories the like of which have never been seen in the history of Europe. 'I did not become a general in the army,' he said later, 'but I became one in literature.'

By the time he was approaching the age of fifty, and coming to the end of *Anna Karenina*, his life, one might suppose, had been a prodigious success. He was rich and famous. By their own noisy standards, he and his wife were still happy together. 'I love it when she is angry with me', he wrote in the first year of his marriage, and this curious taste only began seriously to lose its edge after some twenty years of sensual and intellectual harmony. But all was not well in Tolstoy's life. He was obsessed by death, both fascinated and appalled by the thought of his own extinction. Like Anna Karenina herself, Tolstoy was tugged between two quite contradictory forces: an overwhelming sense within himself of vitality, of life itself (Anna, we are told, was overfilled, crammed with existence, 'too eager to live'); on the other hand, like Anna, Tolstoy was bogged down by life's pointlessness, by its tediousness and its tragedy. As he wrote and rewrote the essentially irrational drama of how Anna made away with herself, he himself became suicidal. We can only speculate as to the *reasons* why the crisis in Tolstoy's life took place at this juncture. Some would say that things were going badly in his marriage, but it would be equally true to say that things went badly with his wife because of his haunting spiritual obsessions, rather than the other way around. Evidently *Anna Karenina* took it out of Tolstoy in a way that *War and Peace* had not. He was imaginatively exhausted by the book. He had put vast quantities of himself into it, and he was left empty, expended, half dead. 'Very well – you will be more famous than Gogol or Pushkin or Shakespeare or Molière, or than all the writers in the world', he took to saying to himself as he paced about the muddy farms, the wretched villages, the fields and copses of his estates. 'So what?'[4]

He tells us in his *Confession*, from which an extract is printed here, that he came out of this crisis as a result of a religious experience. Human life seemed like a remorseless stream, bearing all its sons away. There was nothing to do, it had seemed formerly, but to submit to the tide and be swept on towards nothingness. But then the simple thought had occurred to him. There was something stable, and strong, and still. One could swim for the bank. And the bank was God. Thereafter, though his life knew many tempestuous ups and downs and was shot through with tragedy, Tolstoy never lost this sense of God. Each day would begin with prayer and meditation, and it is quite wrong to think of Tolstoy's religion as a purely ethical or 'rationalist' affair. 'O God, the God who may not be understood, but who art, O God, by whose will I live! Thou hast placed within me the aspiration to know Thee and to know myself. I have gone astray. I have sought the truth where it could not be found. I knew that I was deceiving myself. I have given myself up to evil passions, while knowing that they were evil. Yet never did I forget Thee. I was always conscious of Thy presence, even in the very moment of my errors. I would have perished by losing Thee, but Thou hast offered me a hand which I have seized, and all my life has been filled with light. . . .'[5]

This prayer comes into a work which some Christians would inevitably find contentious, a long book called *A Critique of Dogmatic Theology*. It represents a very lively faith in a personal creator, but it appears in a context which is less than sympathetic to orthodox (small or large 'O') Christianity.

Tolstoy had in part been led to the conversion which saved his life by observing the lives of the peasants, and the happy fervour of their religion.

With his zest for self-dramatization, he immediately threw himself into the role of a pious *muzhik*, losing no opportunity to attend the Divine Liturgy, to fast, to strike the floor and to strike his breast, to invoke God, His angels and His saints. It apparently did not occur to Tolstoy in the first instance that if there is a personal God, He would not call us to worship Him in another man's way, only in our own way. Nor, with Tolstoy's life-long desire (part Marie Antoinette, part modern egalitarian) to live like a peasant, would it have occurred to him that – since religion touches our deepest aspirations, yearnings and needs, all the workings of the brain and heart – what satisfied an illiterate peasant would be highly unlikely to nourish for long so intelligent and inquiring a temperament as his own. He took to visiting the famous monasteries of Russia – in particular the Optina Monastery (which Dostoevsky immortalized in *The Brothers Karamazov*) and to studying the Scriptures, and the early history of Christianity.

The nineteenth century is spattered with Christians who 'lost their faith' by searching into these questions. In the West, whether one thinks of the Protestant tradition of Tübingen and Strauss's *Lebenjesu*, or of the Catholic sceptics like Renan or Loisy, the whole thing appeared to hang on questions of historical authenticity. Such great works in German as Harnack's *History of Dogma* represents the classic 'modernist' view that orthodox Christian theology is a 'development' of a simple primitive Gospel; that the Councils and Creeds, with their carefully defined Christology, were propounding a view of the person of Christ which would have astonished Christ Himself; that the documents of the New Testament were much later, and much more full of contradictions, than anyone had ever before dared to suppose, etc., etc. Indeed it was part of John Henry Newman's genius to absorb this idea and, as it were, to 'bag' it for the Church.

Tolstoy had a voracious capacity for 'getting up' a subject. His Greek (which he had learnt a few years previously in order to read Homer) was good, and he read the works of the progressive French and German writers. He did not think highly of them, and his attitude is revealed clearly by a letter to his friend N. N. Strakhov of April 1878. He condemns Renan's *Vie de Jesus* for two reasons:

> If Renan had any ideas of his own, they are the two following ones:
>
> (1) that Christ didn't know about *l'évolution et le progrès*, and in this respect Renan tries to correct him and criticize him from the superior position of this idea. This is terrible, at least to me. Progress in my opinion is a logarithm of time, i.e. nothing, an establishment of the fact that we live in time; and suddenly it becomes the judge of the highest truth we know. . . .
>
> The other new idea of Renan's is that if Christ's teaching exists then some man or other existed, and this man certainly sweated and went to the lavatory. For us all degrading realistic human details have disappeared from Christianity for the same reason that all details about all Jews etc., who have ever lived have disappeared, for the same reason that everything disappears that is not everlasting; but what is everlasting remains. . . .[6]

It is what is everlasting which dominates Tolstoy's thought. He is one of those geniuses with an eye for the obvious – but an obvious which the rest of us can miss. An extraordinary proportion of religious controversy in the nineteenth century was concerned with the question of whether Jesus really lived, if so whether he could perform miracles, whether he was divine, etc. And fury raged on both sides of the controversy. But neither side paused to ask: Are the teachings of Jesus true? Should we be living in the way Jesus taught?

Tolstoy became convinced of the truth that he had always felt in his heart, that the teachings of Jesus in the gospels provide the key of how a good human life should be lived in this world. He drew up his own selection of New Testament writings designed to emphasize these teachings, and removed the stories of the miracles and the resurrection. If Renan's Jesus was a sentimental Breton, who loved his mother and enjoyed picking flowers, Tolstoy's Jesus is a rather peppery country gentleman with an aristocratic disdain for bureaucrats, Europeanizers, Tsars, Procurators, bishops and the like. Tolstoy gets rid of all the elements in the Gospel which do not make sense, and thereby changes its very nature. No one here kneels in awe before a transfigured Christ on Tabor; no one sees Him still the winds and the waves; no women flee, terrified in the darkness of dawn, at the discovery of an empty tomb. Instead, there is the country gentleman teaching his *muzhiks* how to live, and there are the bishops and clergy who are too hypocritical or too stupid to see the plain truth.

Some modern Western readers of Tolstoy, and all Eastern Christians, who read his religious writings today will find their exaggerations and errors, their omissions and distortions, quite manifest. And they might be therefore inclined to dismiss Tolstoy altogether as some sort of crackpot, interesting as an eccentric sideshow in the nineteenth-century religious history, and in his own sphere a genius, but on the question of the gospels little more than a bad joke.

The attitude of the Orthodox Church to Tolstoy in his own lifetime – an attitude which culminated in his excommunication – makes it much less easy to dismiss Tolstoy like this. After all, if you are a modernist or a half-believer, there is every reason why you might think that you could let yourself off the more searching moral demands of Jesus. Jesus told us that we should refuse to resist evil, but accept it; even if someone hits us in the face, we must turn the other cheek; Jesus taught not merely that we should be sexually restrained, but that anyone looking at a woman to lust after her has already committed adultery; Jesus told us not to lay up treasure on earth. He did not say, 'Be moderate in your accumulations of capital' – he preached a way of dispossession. Jesus forbade his followers to take oaths.

Tolstoy, like St Francis of Assisi six centuries earlier, was revolutionary enough to think that when Jesus taught these things, He might actually have meant them. It was understandable that agnostic liberals like Turgenev should have viewed with a mixture of horror and amusement Tolstoy's attempt to fashion his life according to the Gospel precepts. He tried to dispossess himself; he preached the Christian doctrine of pacifism; he struggled against anger and lust. We would not expect sympathy from those who did not believe Jesus to have any unique claim upon our loyalty. But what of those whose Church was founded in Jesus's name, and who proclaimed – what Tolstoy could not – that Jesus was not merely a teacher inspired by God, but Very God of Very God? They, presumably, would be much more fervent in their desire to live according to the gospels than a 'freelance' Christian such as Tolstoy himself.

As every reader of nineteenth-century history knows, the Orthodox Church was proudly and inescapably bound up with the autocracy of the Emperor. In the name of Jesus, who taught that we should not resist our enemies, Orthodox metropolitans blessed the Holy Orthodox armies. In the name of Jesus, who taught us not to take oaths, an Orthodox priest swore in the witnesses before the trial of criminals. Here – in the broken English of an exile, a religious dissident of the 1890s, who had himself suffered in one of the notorious penal battalions reserved for those who refused military service on religious grounds – is an account of the persecutions which he witnessed:

> From the very first day the bloody chastisement commenced. They were flogged with thorny rods, whose thorns were remaining in the flesh, and thrown in a cold and dark cell afterwards. After a few days they were requested again to do the service, and for the refusal flogged again. And so it was going on and no end was seen. Besides they were always hungry, because they were eating no meat and were given too

little bread. They were physically exhausted; many were sick; but the doctor was refusing to admit them to hospital, unless they would agree to eat meat. The chaplain was requiring the performance of Orthodox rites, and they were driven to the church by fists and musket butt-ends. . . .[7]

When we read Tolstoy's strictures on the Orthodox Church, and feel inclined to protest at, for example, the crude lampooning of the Liturgy in *Resurrection*, we should remember scenes like this. Tolstoy was not attacking the Russian Orthodox Church as we know it today, a suffering, noble, spiritual church. He was attacking the brocaded arm of a tyrannical regime, a church whose clergy were ignorant and corrupt, and whose bishops were little more than pawns of the state.

Yet it is in his attitude to the state, rather than to the Church, that Tolstoy will probably find the greatest number of dissenters from his point of view. To my mind, his distrust of all forms of government is at once the most attractive and the least acceptable aspect of his religious thought, but I would not expect it to find much of an echo either in the bosoms of the Orthodox, or of those Western Christians who believe that the Church is most itself when advising governments on their foreign, fiscal or domestic policies. The Western reader might well be revolted by Tolstoy's anarchism, until he reminded himself of what it was in Orthodoxy against which Tolstoy was reacting.

Tolstoy's anarchism, which became more and more extreme as the years progressed, was particularly addressed to the ears of his Orthodox hearers. In the various legends on which the Western mind likes to focus – whether of Becket and Henry II, or More and Henry VIII, or Innocent XI or Pascal versus the Bourbon monarchy – the interest of civil rulers in ecclesiastical affairs is seen as *interference*. The ideal Christian Church, it is felt, is one where the secular authority has no control, and the very notion that kings or doges might have a say in the running of the Church is seen as 'Erastian' by Western Christians. The Kirchenkampf in Germany in the 1930s was but the culmination in the West of a whole series of confrontations which had been going on ever since the days of Hildebrand between the civil and the ecclesiastical powers.

But the East had fed its mind on different stories. The first

Christian city, Tsarogorod, or Constantinople, had, like the first Ecumenical Council of the Church at Nicaea, come into being through the decree of a Christian Emperor. Constantine, in Western eyes a figure who symbolizes a compromising of a Gospel which is not of this world, is in the East revered as a saint. It was he who made the Empire Christian. His cult derives from an idea of *power* which is found in the New Testament, that strand of thought which bids us render to Caesar the things which are Caesar's and to submit ourselves to every ordinance of man for the Lord's sake. 'The powers that be', wrote the apostle Paul during the reign of the Emperor Nero, 'are ordained of God.' If this were true of a pagan Caesar, how much truer it must have been of the potentate who founded Christendom itself. Equally was it true, in Russian eyes, of the monarch of old Russ, whose conversion to Byzantine Christianity in 988 marked the beginning of 'Holy Russia'. Vladimir, like the Emperor Constantine, bears the title *Isapostolus*, which means 'equal to an apostle'. In the West, the majority of monarch-saints are martyrs, or those who have somehow failed to exercise their monarchical authority. It was easier to be canonized in the East just for being a king. The Eastern churches have a less narrowly sacerdotal vision of humanity than those of the Latin rite. All believers, for the Orthodox, are kings and priests. Christian kings, princes and governors, no less than bishops, are God's ministers. Since all power belongs to God and comes from God, there can be nothing wrong, by this view, in allowing the secular authority to exercise power even in the ecclesiastical sphere. So, in nineteenth-century Russia, it was a layman who was Procurator of the Holy Synod, and the Tsar who decided even doctrinal matters. In 1842, the Procurator was a retired army officer called Pratasov, who was able to forbid the Metropolitan of Moscow to prepare a commentary on the Holy Scriptures. Nicholas I, himself only an army officer with no theological training, was consulted about the after-life and decreed, rather to the consternation of his clergy, that there was no purgatory. Nevertheless, to the Orthodox the stubbornness or ignorance of the laity is no more or less troubling than that of the clergy. And Eastern believers have looked askance at the various attempts at theocracy in the history of the West where, in their suspicion of 'Christian kings, princes and governors', clergymen have seized for themselves a secular influence, and created such unevangelical anomalies as the state of Geneva under Calvin or the quasi-imperial pomps of the Vatican. Tolstoy was no doubt reacting against the corruption and abuse which he deemed to have overcome the court and the Church in nineteenth-century Russia. But his anarchistic distrust of civil authority *per se* is deeply and deliberately unRussian. In his devotion to the Beatitudes, in his pacificism, in his distrust of material possessions and his desire to live like a beggar and a pilgrim, it is almost possible to believe that Tolstoy drew unconscious inspiration from the traditions of Russian Orthodoxy. But the anarchism is not a native flowering. It is all of a piece with his fierce independence of mind and his exaggerated sense of self. It was fed from a variety of sources – from Rousseau, from Proudhon, as well as from the American sectaries with whom he was in correspondence, most especially from the Quakers.

It also has to be said that, as well as being the least Russian, it is also the silliest of his teachings. Neither common-sense, nor the New Testament (and the two are not always coincident) suggest to us that civil government is in itself an evil. No one would deny that Christ came to found a Kingdom not of this world. But it is from Proudhon and not from Christ that Tolstoy derives his belief that all governments are of necessity founded upon violence. And one is bound to ask – since Tolstoy never really supplies an answer – why Christianity should necessarily consider it sinful to supply a populace with food, roads and drains, none of which, in the history of mankind, have ever been available without the intervention of some centralized authority. Tolstoy's reasons for doubting the validity of civil defence, not to mention wars or prisons, are explained very fully in his writings, though his failure to distinguish between the violence of an individual (which Christianity has always condemned) and a magistrate's duty to defend the defenceless citizen, stems directly from his anarchic understanding of The State. One has to add that when hunger befell Russia in 1891 he would immediately lay aside his anarchistic principles and become once more the authoritative officer-type, organizing relief on a huge scale. Likewise, his objection to owning his own copyrights was forgotten when he wished to raise money to give religious dissidents safe conduct to the New World. The virtue of Tolstoy's deeds quite often belied the absurdity of his attitudes. And one should remember this when reading his religious stuff.

Healthy, then, as it might be that governments should always have vociferous thorns in their side, it is impossible to believe in Tolstoy's position of religious anarchism. Perhaps the error of it springs from his fundamental theological inability to understand the Incarnation. His religion was ultimately a thing of the Law rather than of Grace, a scheme for human betterment rather than a vision of God penetrating a fallen world. The contrast between Tolstoy and mainstream Christianity is vividly brought out by the dilemmas facing the German Church during the Kirchenkampf, and the theology, as well as the moral problems, which grew out of that. Tolstoy was resisting a government which was in name Christian, and trying to persuade them that such a thing was a contradiction in terms. In the face of a civil authority as powerful and as manifestly evil as the Third Reich, did not a Christian's duty lie in *doing* something, even in doing something of itself sinful, such as murdering Hitler, for the sake of the millions whom he was causing to suffer? Out of this dilemma came the life and theology of Pastor Bonhoeffer whose book *Ethics* provides the best criticism I know of the sort of position which so tempted Tolstoy.

> Jesus took upon Himself the guilt of all men, and for that reason every man who acts responsibly becomes guilty. If any man tries to escape guilt in responsibility he detaches himself from the ultimate reality of human existence, and what is more he cuts himself off from the redeeming mystery of Christ's bearing guilt without sin, and he has no share in the divine justification which lies upon this event. He sets his own personal innocence above his responsibility for men, and he is blind to the more irredeemable guilt which he incurs precisely in this. . . .[8]

This hits off precisely what is wrong with Tolstoy's position (although Bonhoeffer was not writing about Tolstoy) and is a strange illustration of the paradox that theology which appears to be fantastical is actually realistic. Tolstoy would have dismissed the idea of Christ bearing our guilt as a meaningless dream buzzing in the mind of St Paul (whom he hated). It is much more seemingly rational merely to limit yourself to practising the ideals of Christ, and to abandon the 'meaningless' old ideas of salvation and incarnation. Yet it is the old ideas which create a realistic and living picture of our world. The new purely ethical Christianity began by being impracticable (witness the failure of all the so-called Tolstoyan communities which started up in the early years of this century) and ends by leaving behind the spirit of Christ. By the end of his days, Tolstoy was no less religious but he felt detached from Christianity. When someone told him that a German had written a book proving that Jesus did not exist, he just shrugged, as though the historical existence of Jesus was of no interest to him. He begged his wife to let him leave home, and live in a hut and die like an old Hindu. 'All is vanity. All is falsehood, except that infinite sky.'

But that is not the whole of Tolstoy. No one can ignore Tolstoy's great achievement as a Christian writer. On the one hand he had the power endlessly to provoke us and to annoy us by challenging us with the very words of Christ Himself. If we truly took to heart the Sermon on the Mount and the other teachings of Jesus, would we live as we are living? Would society be ordered, or disordered, as it is? Would we expect governments of the kind we have if we seriously believed in the Gospel? Very often, we shall find that our Christian conscience forces us to side with the 'heretic' Tolstoy against our preconceived picture of property, the military, or of crime and punishment.

Secondly, a much bigger thing. We revere Tolstoy, not just as a prophet but as one of the greatest artists. His art and his thought are all of a piece, and they are both profoundly expressive of true Christian liberty, the liberty which comes of recognizing that we are all individuals made in God's image and likeness. This inheritance is described very well by Dr Zhivago in Pasternak's novel:

> The gospels are an offer, a naïve and tentative offer: 'Would you like to live in a completely new way? Would you like to enjoy spiritual beatitude?' And everybody was delighted, they all accepted and were carried away by it for thousands of years. . . .
>
> 'When the gospels say that in the Kingdom of God there are neither Jews nor Gentiles, do they just mean that all are equal in the sight of God? I don't believe it means only that – that was known already – it was known to the Greek philosophers and the Roman

moralists and the Hebrew Prophets. What the gospels tell us is that in this new way of life and of communion, which is born of the heart and which is called the Kingdom of God, there are no nations, but only persons.

'Now you said that facts don't mean anything by themselves – not until a meaning is put into them. Well – the meaning you have to put into the facts to make them relevant to human beings is just that: it's Christianity, it's the mystery of personality.'[9]

It was in his novels and short stories that Tolstoy could best explore this mystery. It is in those works that he lives. But the non-fictional works are on occasion equally expressive of that mystery; and few personalities were ever more mysterious than his own.

Notes

1. *Why Do Men Stupefy Themselves?*, The Jubilee Edition of Tolstoy's Complete Works, Volume 27, pp. 281–5.

2. *War and Peace*, Book III, p. xiii.

3. *Tolstoy's Diaries* (ed. R. F. Christian), The Athlone Press 1985, p. 101.

4. *Confession*, Jubilee Edition, Volume 23, p. 44.

5. *A Critique of Dogmatic Theology*, Jubilee Edition, Volume 25, p. 187.

6. *Tolstoy's Letters* (ed. R. F. Christian), The Athlone Press 1978, p. 322.

7. *The Doukhobors*, George Woodcock and Ivan Avakumovic, O.U.P. 1968, p. 98.

8. Dietrich Bonhoeffer, *Ethics*, S.C.M. Press 1955, p. 210.

9. Boris Pasternak, *Doctor Zhivago*, Collins 1958, p. 117.

A Confession

Between 1862, when he got married, and 1877, Tolstoy was occupied with many absorbing concerns: with family life (his wife gave birth to nine children in this period); with farming; with the education of his peasants in the school which he had founded on his estate at Yasnaya Polyana. But above all, he was absorbed in fiction.

The years 1862 to 1869 were dominated by the writing and rewriting of *War and Peace*. When he had finished this novel he suffered an experience of appalling psychological terror in which he felt himself confronted by Death.

But the feeling passed. Tolstoy threw himself into his many varied activities and, with the enormous fortune he earned from *War and Peace*, he expanded his estates and bought 67,000 acres in the remote district of Samara, where he enjoyed the company of, among others, a sect called the Molokans – a group of Bible Christians, named after the ass's milk which they liked to consume, who did not accept the rites and ceremonies of the Orthodox Church.

From the early 1870s onwards, Tolstoy began to work on the idea of *Anna Karenina*. His most intense period of work on the book was from 1874 to 1877, when it was finished. After *Anna Karenina*, as after *War and Peace*, he suffered spiritual depletion, moral exhaustion, and psychological horror. He became obsessed by death.

The horror of this period was abated by Tolstoy's rediscovery of religious faith. His *Confession*, in which he describes this vitally important period of his life, was probably written in 1879, when he had already abandoned his short spell of practising Russian Orthodoxy and come to a simple belief in what he thought of as New Testament Christianity, much like that of his friends the Molokans. Only not really like, because in all Tolstoy's religious writings one hears that controversial tone which had coloured the theoretical passages of *War and Peace*, and which proclaim him, for all his sentimental attachment to Russian peasants and their simplicities, every inch a European intellectual and an heir to the Enlightenment.

A Confession

CHAPTER TWELVE

The awareness of the failure of rational knowledge helped to free me from the temptation of idle philosophizing. The conviction that the knowledge of truth can be found only in one way, through life, led me to doubt the rightness of my own life; what truly saved me, however, was that I managed to break free from my own exclusive circle, to see the life of the simple working people, and to understand that this alone can be called real life. I understood that, if I am to understand life and its meaning, I must live a real life rather than that of a parasite. I understood that I must accept the meaning given to life by real humanity, merge with this life, and so verify its meaning.

At this time something happened to me. During this year, when I was wondering almost every minute whether to end it all with a noose or a bullet – during all this time, while my mind was full of the thoughts and observations I have described above, my heart was filled with a heavy ache. I can only describe this ache as the search for God.

I say that this search for God was a feeling, rather than a rational thought, because it emerged not from my process of reasoning – which it in fact directly contradicted – but from my heart. It was a sense of terror, of being orphaned, of isolation in an alien world, and a hope of help from someone unknown.

Although I was quite convinced of the impossibility of proving the existence of God (Kant had shown this and I fully understood his reasoning), I was still seeking God, hoping that I would find Him and addressing prayers out of habit to Him I sought but could not find. I went over in my mind the arguments of Kant and Schopenhauer showing the impossibility of proving the existence of God, and at the same time I began to refute them. Cause, I said to myself, is a different category of thought from Space or Time. If I exist, then there is a cause for that and a cause for all causes. And this cause of everything is what is called God; I stayed with this thought and I attempted with my whole being to be aware of the presence of this cause. As soon as I recognized that there is a power to which I am subordinate, then I began to sense the possibility of life. But I kept asking myself, 'What is this power, this cause? How should I think about it? How should I relate to what I call God?' The only answers that occurred to me were very familiar ones: 'He is the Creator and Preserver.' I was not satisfied by such answers and I felt that something vital to me was being lost. I was appalled and began to pray to Him I was seeking, begging Him to help me. The more I prayed, the more obvious it became that He did not hear me and that there was no one to whom I could turn. My heart now full of despair that there was no God at all, I repeated: 'Lord have mercy upon me, save me! Lord, my God, teach me!' But no one had mercy upon me and I felt that my life was coming to a standstill.

But again and again I came by different ways to the realization that I could not have appeared in the world without any cause, reason or meaning; that I could not really be what I felt myself to be, a fledgling that had fallen from the nest. And even if I were a fledgling, lying on my back and crying in the tall grass, then I was crying because I knew that my mother had borne me, hatched me, warmed me, fed me and loved me. Where was this mother of mine? If I had been abandoned, then who by? I could not hide from the fact that someone had loved me and given birth to me. But who was this someone? – God.

'He knows; He sees my searching, my despair, my struggle. He exists', I said to myself. I only had to admit this momentarily for life to rise up within me, for me to feel the possibility and joy of being. But again I went on from acknowledging the existence of God to looking for a way of relating to Him – and again I imagined the same God the Creator, in three persons, who sent His own son to be our redeemer. And once again this God – a God who was separate from both me and the world as a whole – melted in front of my eyes like a block of ice until nothing was left of Him; my source of life dried up and I fell into despair, thinking there was nothing left but to kill myself. And the worst thing of all was that I felt quite unable to do this.

All this happened to me not two or three times, but dozens and hundreds of times – a sense of joy and animation, followed by despair and a feeling that life was impossible.

Once, in early Spring, I remember being alone in a forest and listening to the various sounds. As I listened, I thought of what I had been thinking about constantly for the preceding three years. I was again searching for God.

'Very good, there is no God', I said to myself. 'There is no God who is not just an imaginary figure, but something as real as my own life. And nothing, no miracle, can prove the opposite – since miracles are irrational, just an effect of the imagination.'

'But what about my conception of the God I am looking for?', I asked myself. 'Where has that come from?' With this thought I once again felt the glad waves of life rise up within me. Everything around me came to life and took on meaning. But this joy of mine did not last for long; my mind was already carrying out its work. 'An idea of God', I said to myself, 'is not the same as God. An idea is something within me, an idea of God is something within me that I can call up or not call up. And that is not what I am looking for. I am looking for something without which there could be no life.' Once again everything around and within me began to die; once again I wanted to kill myself.

Then I looked at myself and what was happening in me. I remembered all the hundreds of times I had died and then come to life again. I remembered that I only lived when I believed in God. 'As before, so now', I said to myself. 'I need only be aware of God and I live; I need only forget Him, or cease to believe in Him, and I die. What is all this dying and coming to life? I do not live when I lose faith in the existence of God; but for my dim hope of finding Him I would have killed myself long ago. I live, truly live, only when I feel Him and search for Him. So what else am I seeking for?' cried a voice within me. 'There He is. He is what one cannot live without. To know God is the same thing as to live. God is life.'

'Live in search of God and there will be no more life without God.' Then everything around me and within me lit up, more brightly than ever before, and this light has never again left me.

And so I was saved from suicide. When and how this change occurred I cannot say. My life-force had gradually and imperceptibly been destroyed, I had gradually and imperceptibly come to a standstill in life, a sense that it was impossible to go on living, a need to commit suicide; it was equally gradually and imperceptibly that this life-force returned to me. One strange thing is that this life-force was nothing new, but rather something very old indeed, the same force that had led me through my very first steps in life. I returned in all ways to the things of my childhood and youth. I returned to a faith in a Will that had produced me and now wanted something from me. I returned to the belief that the only aim of my life was to live better, i.e. more in harmony with this Will. I returned to the belief that I can find an expression of this Will in what humanity created for its own guidance in a past that is hidden to me, that is, I returned to a faith in God, in the aspiration towards moral perfection and in a tradition that passed on the meaning of life. The only difference was that in the past I had known all this unconsciously whereas now I knew that without it I was unable to live.

What happened to me is something like this. At a time I can no longer remember I was placed in a boat and pushed off from some unknown shore. Someone pointed me to the far shore, put some oars in my inexperienced hands and then left me on my own. I rowed as best I could, and moved forward; but the nearer I drew to the middle of the river, the more rapid grew the current carrying me away from my goal, and the more other people I met who were also being carried away by it. There were a few people who were continuing to row; there were others who had abandoned their oars; there were large boats and huge ships full of people. Some of these were still struggling against the current; others had yielded to it. The further I went, the more I tended to look downstream, where everyone was being swept, and to forget my own direction. And in the very middle of the river, in the crowd of boats and ships being swept downstream, I entirely lost my direction and abandoned my oars. On all sides people with sails and oars were being carried gaily downstream, cheerfully assuring me and one another that there was no other direction. I believed them and followed. I was carried a long way, so far that I could hear the sound of the rapids where I would have been smashed; I could even see boats that had already been shattered. Then I came back to myself. For a long time I was unable to understand what had happened. All I could see before me was ruin; I was afraid of it, yet still rushing towards it, unable to glimpse any salvation, and not knowing what I should do. Only when I looked back, catching sight of countless boats still obstinately fighting the current, did I remember the shore, my oars and my direction. And so I began to row back, upstream and against the current.

The shore was God, the direction was tradition, and the oars were the freedom I had been granted to row towards the shore, to become one with God. And so the power of life was renewed in me and I once again began to live.

CHAPTER FIFTEEN

How often I envied the peasants their illiteracy and lack of learning. Statements of faith, that to me seemed clearly nonsensical, to them contained nothing false; they were able to accept them and to believe in the truth, the same truth in which I believed. Only it was clear to me, unhappy man that I am, that this truth was closely, through the finest of threads, interwoven with falsehood and that I could not accept it in such a guise.

I lived like this for about three years. At first, when, possessed as I was, I only partook very slightly of truth, when, guided by instinct, I was merely walking where it seemed brighter, these clashes seemed of less account. When I did not under-stand something, I said to myself, 'I am to blame, I am evil'. But the more I became imbued with the truths I was studying, the more they became the foundation of my life, the more difficult and glaring became these clashes – and the clearer the dividing line between what I did not understand because I am unable to understand it and what I could understand only by lying to myself.

In spite of these doubts and sufferings I still held to the Orthodox Church. But then vital questions arose which had to be resolved; and the resolution of these questions by the Church – a resolution that was abhorrent to the very foundation of the faith I lived by – finally compelled me to renounce the possi-bility of communion with Orthodoxy. The most serious of these questions was the attitude of the Orthodox Church to other Churches – to Catholicism and the so-called schismatics. At the time, as a result of my interest in religion, I had grown friendly with believers of various faiths: Catholics, Protestants, Old Believers, Molokans, and others. Among them I had met many people who were both highly moral and truly religious. I wanted to be a brother to them. And what happened? The teaching that had promised to unite everyone in one faith and love – this very teaching, in the person of its best representa-tives, told me that these people were caught in a lie, that what gave them their vital strength was a temptation of the devil, and that we alone possessed the only possible truth. And I saw that all those who do not profess an identical faith are considered by the Orthodox to be heretics – just as the Catholics and other Churches consider the Orthodox themselves to be heretics. I saw that Orthodoxy looks with hostility – though it tries to hide this – on all those who do not profess their faith through the same external words and symbols as it does itself. I saw that this is inevitable: firstly, because this assertion, that I know the truth while you are caught in a lie, is the harshest thing that one man can say to another; and secondly, because a man who loves his children and brothers cannot help but look with hostility on those who wish to convert his children and brothers to a false belief. And this hostility increases in proportion to a man's knowledge of theology. And so it became clear to me, who believed that truth lay in the union of love, that theology itself destroyed what it should be producing.

This temptation is so obvious, so very obvious to us educated people who have lived in countries where various faiths are professed, who have seen the self-assured, unshakeable contempt of the Catholic for the Orthodox and the Protestant, of the Orthodox for the Catholic and the Protestant, and of the Protestant for the two others – not to mention the Old Believers, Pashkovites, Shakers and other sects – that the very obviousness of the temptation is at first a source of perplexity. One says to oneself: it is impossible for it to be so very simple and for people still not to see that if two assertions contradict one another, then neither of them can lay claim to the whole truth which faith should represent. One thinks there must be something else, some other explanation. I thought so myself. I read everything on the subject I could. I spoke to everyone I could. And the only explanation I found was that which makes the Sumsky Hussars consider the finest regiment in the world to be the Sumsky Hussars, and the Yellow Uhlans consider the finest regiment in the world to be the Yellow Uhlans. Ecclesiastics of all the different faiths, their finest representatives, could say only one thing: that they believed that they knew the truth and that the others were in error; and that all they could do was pray for them. I went to ask archimandrites, bishops, elders, monks of the strictest orders – and not one of them made any attempt to explain this temptation to me. And then one of them made everything clear to me, so clear that I never asked anyone else about it again.

I said that for every unbeliever turning towards the faith – and the whole of our younger generation could find themselves in such a position – the first question to be answered is this: Why is the truth not in Lutheranism, not in Catholicism, but in Orthodoxy? Educated in the high school, he cannot remain unaware, like the peasant, that the Protestant and the Catholic affirm with equal conviction that theirs is the only true faith. The evidence of history, distorted by each of the Churches in its own favour, is inadequate. Is it not possible – I asked – to understand the teaching in some higher way, so that from its perspective all differences disappear, as they do for one who believes truly? Is it not possible to proceed further along the same path upon which we have set out with the Old Believers? They said that we have a differently shaped cross, different ways of saying Alleluia, a different way of processing around the altar. We replied, 'You believe in the Nicene Creed and the Seven Sacraments – and so do we. Let us both hold to that, while in other matters you may do as you please.' We were able to unite with them because we valued what is essential in our faith more highly than what is inessential. Is it not possible now for us to say to the Catholics, 'You believe in this and that, in what really matters, and you can do as you please with regard to the *filioque* clause and the Pope'? Is it not possible for us to say the same to the Protestants, uniting with them around what is essential?

The man I was talking to agreed with my thoughts, but told me that such concessions would lead to a schism, bringing criticism on the heads of the spiritual authorities for deserting the faith of our forefathers – when their calling is to preserve the Graeco-Russian Orthodox faith in all its purity.

At that moment I understood everything. I was searching for faith, for vital strength, while they were looking for the best way to fulfil certain human obligations to other people. And they fulfil these human obligations in a very human way. Whatever they say about their compassion for their erring brethren, about the prayers they repeat on their behalf which rise up to the throne of the Almighty, it is impossible to achieve human purposes without violence; it always has been used, is used now and always will be used. If each of two faiths believes itself to be correct and the other to be false, then their adherents will preach their doctrines, hoping to bring the others to the truth. And if a false doctrine is preached to the inexperienced sons of the true Church, then this Church cannot help but burn books and remove the man who is tempting its sons. What is to be done with this sectarian – who ardently believes in a faith the Orthodox believe to be false and who is misleading the sons of the Church with regard to the most important matter in life, with regard to faith? What else can be done with him but to chop off his head or to lock him up? Under Tsar Alexey Mikhailovich such people were burnt at the stake; in our day they still undergo the most severe form of punishment – which is now solitary confinement. And so, as I thought about what is perpetrated in the name of religion, I was appalled; indeed, I almost reached the point of abjuring Orthodoxy.

The second question of vital importance where I found myself in disagreement with the Church was that of war and capital punishment. At that time Russia was at war. In the name of Christian love, Russians began to kill their fellow men. It was impossible not to think about this, impossible not to see that murder is an evil abhorrent to the very foundations of any faith. But at the same time prayers were being said in the churches for the success of our arms; our spiritual teachers even saw this killing as an expression of faith. Nor was it only a matter of murders committed during the war; I saw church dignitaries, teachers and monks give their approval to the murder of lost and helpless young men during the disturbances that took place after the war. Yes, as I thought about what is done by those who profess Christianity, I was appalled.

CHAPTER SIXTEEN

I no longer doubted; I was now fully convinced that not all was true in the faith which I had joined. Earlier I would have said that it was all false, but now I could no longer say that. The whole of the people possessed a knowledge of truth; this was indisputable, since without this knowledge they could not have gone on living. More than that, I had already come to share in this knowledge of truth; I already lived by it and was able to sense its reality. But this knowledge also contained a measure of falsehood; of that there could be no doubt. And all that had previously repelled me now stood vividly before me. Although I could see that among the people as a whole there was a smaller measure of the falsehood I found so abhorrent than among the representatives of the Church, it was clear that their truth was indeed still adulterated with falsehood.

But where had this falsehood and this truth first come from? They had both of them been handed down by what we call the Church. They were both contained in tradition, in the so-called holy tradition and in the Scriptures.

And so, against my will, I was led to the study of these writings and traditions, a study of which until then I had been afraid. I turned to the study of the same theology which I had once so scornfully dismissed as irrelevant. At a time when I was surrounded on all sides by manifestations of life which seemed clear and full of meaning, I had thought of it as a series of irrelevant absurdities; even now I would be glad to throw out any thought that cannot be entertained by a sound mind – but what can I do? The only knowledge of the meaning of life I have ever found is based on this teaching, or at the very least is inseparably linked with it. However far-fetched it may seem to my old sober mind, it is my only hope of salvation. I must examine it carefully and attentively in order to understand it – though not, of course, in the way that I understand a proposition of science. I am not seeking that, nor, knowing the special character of religious knowledge, can I ever do so. I shall not look for explanations of it. I know that the explanation of everything, like the beginning of everything, cannot but be concealed in infinity. But I want to understand until I am brought up against what is inevitably inexplicable; I want what is inexplicable to be so not because the demands of my reason are unjust (they are just and I cannot hope to understand anything without them), but because I can see the limits of my reason. I want to understand in such a way that every inexplicable proposition should seem necessarily inexplicable, not merely something I am under an obligation to believe.

That there is truth in the teaching I am certain, but I am equally certain that there is falsehood. I must find both and distinguish the one from the other. I am now setting to work on this. What I find to be false in the teaching, what I find to be true, and what conclusions I reach – all this will form the following parts of a work which, if it appears to be of value to anyone, will probably one day be printed somewhere or other.

What I Believe

Tolstoy was working on *What I Believe* during the
summer of 1883, when he was fifty-five years old. Like
nearly all Tolstoy's religious writings, it was censored
in Russia, but enjoyed popularity on the underground
presses and in foreign translations. In 1877, Tolstoy's
friend Vladimir Grigorovich Chertkov made a visit to
England, and presented a copy of the book to the poet
Matthew Arnold, who had helped to show Tolstoy
Board Schools in 1861. Arnold was one of the first
Westerners to write intelligently about Tolstoy. *What I
Believe* is a reassertion of Tolstoy's belief in the teachings of Jesus, but not in the doctrines of the Church.
This particular emphasis lays stress on the unmistak-
able pacifist teaching of Christ, which was to
revolutionize Tolstoy's already jaded and suspicious
view not just of war but of all forms of government
which needed violence for their maintenance or pro-
tection. His understanding of Jesus led him, in the
end, to a sort of social anarchism. The story here of
Tolstoy's confrontation with the grenadier at the
Borovitsky gate is typical of his methods of putting
over a case. He is the Socrates who is not afraid of
asking devastatingly simple questions to which we do
not always want to give an answer.

What I Believe

When I understood that the words 'Resist not evil' did indeed mean 'Resist not evil', my whole understanding of Christ's teaching was suddenly changed; I was appalled at the peculiar way in which I had understood it until then. I knew – we all know – that the meaning of the Christian teaching lies in love for other people. To say, 'Turn your cheek, love your enemies', is to express the very essence of Christianity. I had known all this since childhood, but why had I not understood these straight-forward words in a straightforward manner? Why had I searched instead for some allegorical meaning in them? 'Do not resist him that is evil' means 'Do not ever resist him that is evil, do not commit acts of violence, acts that are contrary to the spirit of love.' And if you are insulted, then suffer the insult and still do not commit acts of violence. It is impossible to say any of this more clearly and straightforwardly than Christ did. How could I, who believed, or at least tried to believe, that the man who had said these words was God – how could I say that I lacked the strength to act on these words? It is as though my master were to say, 'Go and chop wood', and I were to reply that I did not have the strength. Such a reply means either that I don't believe what my master says, or that I do not want to do what he tells me. I said with regard to the commandment of God of which He said, 'Whoso doeth this and teacheth men so shall be called great', of which He said that only those who fulfilled it should receive life, which He Himself fulfilled and which He expressed so clearly and straightforwardly as to leave no room whatsoever for doubt – I, who had never even attemp-ted to fulfil it, said of this commandment of God, 'It is impos-

sible for me to fulfil it by my own strength alone, I need supernatural help.'

God came down to earth so as to bring salvation to men. The
Second Person of the Trinity, God the Son, suffered on behalf of
people, redeemed their sins before the Father and gave them
the Church which is the vessel for the grace that is transmitted
to all believers. As well as this, however, God gave people for
their salvation a teaching and the example of His own life. How
could I say that the rule of life He gave so simply and so clearly
to all men was so difficult as to be impossible to follow without
supernatural help? Not only did He not say that, but He said,
'Fulfil this commandment. If you do not fulfil it, you will not
enter the Kingdom of Heaven.' And He never said that it was
difficult to fulfil. On the contrary, He said, 'My yoke is easy, my
burden is light.' John the Evangelist said, 'His commandments
are not hard.' How could I say that what God had told us to do,
what He had described so clearly, what He had said was so
easy, what He Himself had done as a man and what His first
followers had done – how could I say that this was so difficult as
to be impossible without supernatural help? If a man were to
apply all the powers of his intellect to destroying a particular
law, what more damning words could he find than that the law
was impracticable, that the maker of the law knew it was
impracticable and that one needed supernatural help in order
to keep to it? And all this is what I myself thought with regard to
the commandment of non-resistance to evil. I tried to
remember just how and why the strange idea had entered my
head that Christ's law was divine but impossible to fulfil. As I
went through my past, I realized that this thought had never
been imparted to me so starkly, but that I had absorbed it
unconsciously from my earliest childhood and that the rest of
my life had only served to confirm me in this strange delusion.

From childhood I had been taught that Christ was God and
His teaching divine, but I had also been taught to respect the
institutions which used violence to insure my safety from evil
people. I had even been taught to see these institutions as holy.
I was taught that it was shameful and degrading to submit to a

doer of evil, to suffer under him, and that it was praiseworthy to resist him. I was taught to judge and to punish. Then I was taught to be a soldier, that is, to resist the doers of evil by the act of murder. The army of which I was a member was called a Christ-loving army; its acts were sanctioned by a Christian blessing. From childhood to manhood, I was taught what directly contradicts the law of Christ: to resist someone who injures me and to revenge myself through violence for any insult to myself, my family or my nation. Far from incurring disapproval, these principles were instilled into me; I was taught that they were splendid and in no way contradictory to the law of Christ.

Everything around me, my tranquillity, the security of myself and my family, my property, was based on a law that Christ had repudiated, the law of a tooth for a tooth.

Church teachers taught me that Christ's teaching was divine, that human frailty made it impossible to adhere to, and that only Christ's blessing could enable us to accomplish it. And our whole way of life implied what my secular teachers admitted openly: that Christ's teaching was impracticable, a mere fantasy. Through word and deed they taught what was contrary to it. This admission of the impracticability of the Lord's teachings was instilled into me so gradually, came to seem so normal, and harmonized so completely with my own desires, that I was never aware of the contradiction into which I had fallen. I did not see that it was impossible to profess Christ, the basis of whose teaching was non-resistance to evil, and at one and the same time to work calmly and consciously for the establishment of property, law courts, government and armies; impossible to establish a life that was contradictory to Christ's teaching and at one and the same time to pray to Christ for the fulfilment of the law of forgiveness and non-resistance to evil. What now seems so obvious never even entered my head: that it would be considerably simpler to establish a life on the basis of Christ's law and then – if they are indeed so necessary to our well-being – to pray for law courts, executions and wars.

In the end I realized how my error had arisen: from an

acceptance of Christ in word and a denial of Him in deed.

Non-resistance to evil is the commandment that unifies the whole teaching, but not if it is a mere saying, only if it is a rule that is obligatory for everyone, a law.

It truly is a key that opens everything, but only if it is pushed into the lock. To see this commandment as a mere saying, a saying that cannot be followed without supernatural help, is to destroy the whole of the teaching. And a teaching from which the basic, unifying commandment has been removed cannot seem anything but impossible. To unbelievers it seems simply ridiculous, and it cannot appear otherwise.

We have installed an engine, heated up the boiler, set it in motion, but not attached the transmission belt – this is what we have done to the teaching of Christ by saying that it is possible to be a Christian without fulfilling the commandment of non-resistance to evil.

I was recently reading the fifth chapter of Matthew with a Jewish rabbi. After almost every sentence the rabbi would say, 'That is in the Bible, that is in the Talmud.' He would then indeed show me sayings from the Bible or the Talmud that were indeed extremely similar to the Sermon on the Mount. But when we came to the verse about non-resistance to evil, instead of saying, 'That is in the Talmud too', he simply asked mockingly, 'Is that what Christians do? Do they turn the other cheek?' There was nothing I could answer; I knew that Christians at that time were not only not turning the other cheek, but hitting cheeks that Jews had turned. But I was interested to know whether there was anything similar in the Bible or the Talmud, and so I asked him. 'No, there isn't,' he replied, 'but tell me, do the Christians keep to this law?' By this question he implied that the presence of this law in the Christian code, a law that is not only never followed but even admitted by Christians themselves to be impracticable, was an admission of the irrationality and irrelevance of the whole code. And there was nothing I could answer.

Now that I understand the teaching I can clearly see the strange contradiction I had fallen into. I had accepted Christ as

God and His teaching as divine, and at the same time I had arranged my whole life contrary to this teaching. What else could I do save regard the teaching as impracticable? I professed Christ's teaching in my words, but in my deeds I followed a quite un-Christian teaching, paying homage to the quite un-Christian institutions that surrounded my life on all sides.

The whole of the Old Testament states that the misfortunes of the Jewish people stemmed from their belief in false gods and not in the true God. In I Samuel, chapters 8 and 12, the prophet accuses the people of yet another act of disobedience to God, in addition to their former ones: instead of God, they had appointed a man as their king, and they were expecting him to save them. 'Do not believe in vanity', says Samuel to the people. 'It cannot help you or save you because it is vain. So as not to perish together with your king, you must cling to the one God.'

It was faith in the same 'vanity', the same empty idols, that hid the truth from me. The 'vanity' I was too weak to renounce stood on my path to truth, blocking its light.

The other day I was walking through the Borovitsky gates. An old cripple, a beggar, was sitting in the gateway, a rag wrapped round his ears. I took out my purse to give him something. Just then a manly, ruddy young fellow came running down from the Kremlin, a grenadier in his regimental sheepskin coat. Catching sight of the soldier, the beggar jumped up in a fright and ran off with a limp towards the Alexandrov garden. The grenadier chased after him, but then stopped and began to abuse him for sitting in the gateway even though it was prohibited. I waited in the gateway for the grenadier. When he came up to me, I asked him if he could read.

'Yes, but why?' 'Have you read the gospels?' 'Yes.' 'Have you read, "And who shall feed the hungry?"' I quoted the whole passage. He knew it and listened to it; I could see he felt awkward. Two passers-by also stopped to listen. The grenadier had been efficiently carrying out his duty in driving people away, and obviously felt upset to appear suddenly in the wrong. He was embarrassed and appeared to be looking for an excuse.

Suddenly a light gleamed in his dark, intelligent eyes and he turned to one side as though to walk away. 'And have you read the Service Regulations?' he asked. I said that I had not. 'Then keep your mouth shut', said the grenadier with a victorious toss of the head. He adjusted his coat and walked proudly back to his post.

This grenadier is the only man I have ever met in my entire life who has arrived at a strictly logical resolution of the eternal question which confronted me, and under the present social order confronts everyone who calls himself a Christian.

What Then
Must We Do?

Tolstoy was a countryman, and lived nearly all his life on his country estate at Yasnaya Polyana. When, in later years, the household became overcrowded and noisy, he took to looking for even remoter country places in which to be alone with his thoughts. But throughout his life he made periodic visits to St Petersburg, and more often to Moscow since it was only 130 miles from home. The necessity of getting education for the children made his wife long for a permanent Moscow establishment. Much to Tolstoy's disgust, the Countess got her own way, and established a place for the family in her native city in 1881. Until being made to live there, Tolstoy had never explored Moscow thoroughly. Astonishingly for one so observant, Tolstoy knew nothing of the slums, and his first glimpse of them filled him with fascinated horror and social outrage. The squalor and poverty and ignominy of those condemned to lead the lives of the urban poor excited Tolstoy's keenest pity and indignation against the government. *What Then Must We Do?* begins as a sort of Russian Mayhew, with accounts of how the poor live. It moves on, with typical perverseness, to dismiss any practical solution to the problems of poverty. Tolstoy's constantly reiterated message was that we could not solve the problems of modern life by modern political methods or by economics. Only by allowing all these people back to the land could they be free.

Tolstoy, who had seen more than a little of prostitutes as a young man, was nevertheless scandalized by the position of women in the Moscow slums. He gives an unforgettable and highly Dickensian portrait, for instance, of a cigarette-maker and her daughter. The sight of poor women and girls working disgusted him as much as the sight of rich women evading, as he saw it, their duties to get married and have children. Tolstoy's views of women are, to put it mildly, unenlightened. But you miss the full flavour unless you read them.

What Then
Must We Do?

As the Bible says, Man has been given the law of labour, Woman the law of child-bearing. We may have changed all that with our science, but the law of man and the law of woman remain unchanged – just as the liver remains in its place – and any transgression of them is still inevitably punished by death.

The only difference is that a transgression of the law by all men would be punished by death in a future so immediate that it may be called the present, whereas a transgression of the law by all women would be punished by death in a more distant future. A general infringement of the law by all men would destroy humanity immediately, while its infringement by all women would destroy the following generation. The infringement of the law by some men and women does not destroy the human race, merely depriving the offenders of their status as rational human beings. In some classes, those able to coerce others by force, men have transgressed the law for a long time. This transgression has become more and more widespread and in our time has become a madness. It has even been set up as an ideal, an ideal put forward by Prince Blokhin and shared by Renan and the whole of the educated world: machines will do all the work while people become sybaritic bundles of nerves.

Women have almost never transgressed the law. The only exceptions have been prostitution and isolated cases of abortion. Women in rich circles continued to follow their law even after their men had ceased to follow their own. This is why the women grew stronger and came – rightly – to hold power over men who had infringed the law and so lost their reason.

It is often said that women (Parisian women, childless

women) have become so captivating through their use of the arts of civilization that they have been able to gain power over men through their charm. This is not only unfair, but quite contrary to the truth. It is not the childless woman who has gained power over man but the mother, the mother who has fulfilled her own law while the man has failed to fulfil his. The woman who uses artificial means to remain childless, who captivates men with her curls and her bare shoulders – this woman is far from having gained power over men. On the contrary, she has been perverted by men and fallen to their own level; like them she has abandoned her law and lost the rational meaning of her life. It is this mistake that has given birth to the astonishing nonsense called 'women's rights'. The formula of these rights is as follows: 'You men', says the woman, 'have abandoned your duty of labour, but you want us to continue to bear the burden of our own? No! If that is how things stand, then we can make a pretence of labour just as well as you do in your banks, ministries, universities and academies. We too would like to live only to satisfy our desires, making use of the pretence of a division of labour in order to enjoy what has been produced by others.' And these women do indeed prove that they can carry out the pretence of labour even better than men themselves.

The so-called women's question has arisen, and could only arise, in a society where men have abandoned their duty of labour. Men have only to return to this duty for the question to disappear. A woman who has her own unavoidable labour would never demand the right to share man's work in mines or on fields. She could never have demanded to share in anything except the sham labour of the rich.

The woman of our class was, and still is, stronger than the man not because of her charm or because of her skill in carrying out the same hypocritical pretence of labour as the man; she was strong because she did not evade the law, because she endured the true labour, demanding the utmost effort and the risk of life, from which the man of the wealthy classes had freed himself. But within my own memory woman has begun to fall, to evade her duty, and this fall has gone further and further. After losing her own law, woman has begun to believe that her power lies in her captivating charm or the dexterity with which she is able to carry out the hypocritical pretence of intellectual labour. Children, of course, are a hindrance to both of these. And so science has enabled dozens of means of preventing pregnancy to spread among the richer classes. The women of the wealthy classes have let slip the power they held in their own hands as mothers – and they have done this merely in order to compete with prostitutes on the street. This evil, already wide-spread, spreads further with every day. Soon it will have affected all the women of the wealthy classes. They will then be on the same level as men, and will have lost the essential meaning of their lives. But there is still time.

If only women understood their power and importance. If only they used it for the salvation of their husbands, brothers and children. For the salvation of everyone!

Women mothers of the wealthy classes: the salvation of the people of our world from the evils with which they suffer is in your hands!

Not the women who are concerned only with their waists, bustles and hairdos, with how attractive they are to men, who only against their will, out of carelessness, despairingly give birth to children and then hand them over to wet-nurses; not the women who go to various courses and talk about psycho-motor centres and differentiation, who try to avoid child-bearing since it would hinder the process of stupefaction they call 'development'; but the women and mothers who are in a position to avoid childbirth, yet consciously and without reservation submit to the eternal immutable law, knowing that the hardship and labour of this submission is their life vocation: it is these women and mothers of the wealthy classes in whose hands, more than in those of anyone else, lies the possibility of salvation for the people of our world from the evils that weigh on them. You, women and mothers, who consciously submit to the law of God, you alone in our unhappy, mutilated circle that has lost the semblance of being human, you alone know the true meaning of life in accordance with God's law. You alone can show people by your own example the happiness that lies in submission to the will of God, a happiness they choose to deny to themselves. You alone know the ecstasies and joys that envelop the whole being, the bliss intended for man when he does not evade God's law. You know the happiness of love for your husband, a happiness that does not suddenly come to an end like all others but which forms the beginning of the new happiness of love for your child. You alone, when you are unhesitant in your obedience to the will of God, know not the absurd ceremony, in uniforms and illuminated halls, of what the men of your circle call labour; you alone know the true labour decreed for us by God, together with its true rewards and the bliss it affords.

You know this when, after the joys of love, you wait in trepidation, fear and hope for the torment of pregnancy which will make you ill for nine months and bring you to the verge of death, to unbearable pains and sufferings. You know the conditions of true labour when you wait in joy for the approach, even the intensification, of the terrible torments after which will follow the bliss known to you alone.

You know this when, immediately after these torments, with no break or respite, you begin another round of toil and suffering – that of nursing – and must renounce that most powerful of human needs, the need for sleep, which according to the proverb is 'dearer than father or mother'. Then, for months and years, you do not have one undisturbed night; often you do not sleep for nights on end, pacing about alone, rocking in your numb arms a sick child who is breaking your heart.

And when you do all this, receiving no notice or praise and expecting no reward, when you look on all this not as an achievement but – like the labourer in the gospel parable who came from the field – simply as an obligation that you have carried out, then indeed you will know what is a mere show of labour for the praise of men and what is true labour, the execution of the will of God which you sense in your own heart.

And you know, if you are a true mother, that not only does no one see or praise your labour, not only do they take it quite for granted, not only do the people you work for fail to thank you for your labour, but that often they will reproach and torment you. And you do exactly the same with the next child; once again you suffer, once again you endure the same terrible, unseen labour, once again you expect no reward, and experience the same satisfaction.

If you are such a woman, then neither after two nor twenty children will you say that you have had enough – any more than a fifty-year-old labourer will say he has had enough when he still eats and sleeps and has muscles that demand to be exercised. If you are such a woman, then you will not pass on the burden of nursing and rearing the child to some other woman – any more than a labourer will pass on to someone else a task he has begun and almost finished. You put your life into this work; and so, the greater the work, the fuller and happier your life.

If you are such a woman – and there still are some, to our good fortune – then you will apply the same law that guides you in your own life to the lives of your husband, your children, and everyone close to you. If you are such a woman and you know from your own experience that only selfless, unseen, unrewarded labour, carried out at the risk of one's own life and with the utmost concern for the life of others – that only this affords true satisfaction, then you will make such demands on other people and evaluate their worth by their labour, encouraging your husband to perform such labour and preparing your children for it.

Only a mother who looks on childbirth as an unpleasant accident, who believes the meaning of life to lie in the pleasures of love, creature comforts, education and socializing, will bring up her children to have as many pleasures as possible and as many opportunities as possible of enjoying them. Only such a woman will feed them delicacies, dress them up and provide them with artificial amusements, teaching them – whether male or female – not what will render them capable of selfless and exhausting labour, but what will deliver them from such labour. Only such a woman, who has lost the meaning of her own life, will feel kindly towards the sham labour of a husband who has freed himself from his own duty in order to exploit the labours of others. Only such a woman will choose that kind of husband for her daughters, and will evaluate people not by who they are but by what is attached to them: status, money and the ability to exploit the labours of others.

A true mother, who knows the will of God from her own experience, will prepare her own children to carry it out. Such a woman will suffer if she sees her child over-fed, over-dressed and pampered; she knows that all this will make it difficult for him or her to perform the will of God. Such a mother will teach her son or daughter not what will enable them to avoid labour, but what will enable them best to endure the burden of life. She will not need to ask how to teach and rear her children; she knows the true vocation of men and women, and so she knows what children need to be taught. Not only will such a woman not encourage her husband to perform the sham labour whose only goal is the exploitation of the labour of others, but – more than that – she will look with horror and disgust on an activity that serves as a double temptation for her children.

Such a mother gave birth to her own children and so will nurse her own children. Her first concern will be to feed her children, to sew and wash for them, to sleep with them and to talk with them – because she sees this as her life's work. Such a mother will not seek security for her children through her husband's money or their own diplomas, but will imbue in them the same capacity to sacrifice oneself and carry out the will of God that she recognizes in herself, the same capacity to endure labour even when it endangers one's own life – because she knows that this is the only true security and the only true good. Such a woman will never ask others what she should do; she will know everything and be afraid of nothing.

A man or a childless woman may have doubts as to which path they should follow in order to carry out the will of God, but the path of a woman who has become a mother is clear and well-defined. If she obediently, in all simplicity of heart, follows this path, then she will attain the highest degree of perfection that is possible to us; she will become a star, a guiding light to all people who aspire to good. Only a woman can calmly say, before her death, to Him who sent her into this world, to Him whom she has served by bearing and bringing up children she has loved more than herself – only she can calmly say after carrying out all her duties: 'Now lettest Thou Thy servant depart in peace.' And that is the highest degree of perfection to which, as to the highest good, men can aspire.

Such women, women who fulfil their vocation, hold power even over powerful men; such women mould public opinion and prepare future generations. And so it is they who hold the power to save people from all our present and impending evils.

Yes, women, mothers, in your hands more than in those of anyone else lies the salvation of the world.

On Life

On Life, one of his best extended religious essays, was written in 1887. This little extract provides a tangible link between the later Tolstoy – more interested in preaching than in telling a story – and the earlier story-teller. In both, there is this simple reverence for what is, this child-like excitement at life itself. In the masterpiece of his early years, *Cossacks*, the citified young hero, Olenin, is shamefacedly confronted with the Cossacks who, without taking thought, have more gift for life than he does. Yeroshka, the vast old Cossack rogue who befriends Olenin, tells his young friend that 'When you die, that's it. The grass grows over your head'. He finds something comforting in this – just as the Hebrew Psalmist had done, in the days before the Jews evolved a belief in life after death. You catch a little flavour of this in this extract from *On Life*.

On Life

I think that I shall die and that my life will come to an end; I feel sorry for myself and this thought frightens and torments me. But what will die? What do I feel sorry for? What, speaking quite straightforwardly, am I? In the first place I am flesh. So? Am I sorry for that? Am I afraid on behalf of that? I think not. After all, not one particle of body or substance can ever disappear. It appears that this part of me is provided for, that I have nothing to fear on its behalf. It will be kept safe. No – people say – that's not what I'm sorry for. I'm sorry for myself – Lev Nikolayevich, Ivan Semyonych . . . But then none of us is the person we were twenty years ago, we each become a different person every day. Which of these people am I sorry for? No – people say – that's not what I'm sorry for. I'm sorry for my consciousness, my *I*.

But then your consciousness hasn't always been the same either. It was different a year ago, more different ten years ago, and still more different before that; as far back as you can remember, it has always been changing. What do you like so much about your present consciousness, why are you so upset about losing it? If it had always been the same, then one could understand, but it has never done anything except change. You do not see and cannot find its beginning, yet suddenly you want it to have no end; you want the consciousness that is yours now to remain for ever. You have been on the move ever since you can remember. You don't know how you came into this life, but you know you came as the special *I* which you still are. You travelled and travelled until you were half-way through and then you suddenly dug your heels in, half in joy and half in fright, saying you don't want to go any further because you can't see what's there. You didn't see the place you came from, and yet you arrived; you came in at the entrance, but don't want to leave by the exit.

Your whole life has been a passage through physical existence. You moved on, hurrying to go further, and now you suddenly feel sorry that what you have always been doing is still continuing to happen. You are afraid of the great change that will take place at the time of your physical death; but an equally great change took place at the time of your physical birth, and nothing bad came of that. On the contrary, what came of it was so good that you don't want to part with it.

What can be frightening you? You say you regret your *you*, with its present thoughts and feelings, its present view of the world, its present relationship with the world.

You are afraid of losing your relationship with the world. What is this relationship? What does it consist of?

If it consists of the way you eat, drink, reproduce, build houses and dress, the way you behave towards other people and animals, then every human being, as a rational creature, has such a relationship with life – and it is impossible for this relationship to disappear. There have been, still are, and always will be millions of them; their species is as certain to endure as each particle of matter. The instinct for the preservation of the species is powerfully instilled into all animals; it is something so solid that there is no reason to fear for it. If you are an animal, you have nothing to fear; if you are matter, then you can be still more assured of being eternal.

But if you are afraid of losing what is not animal, then you are afraid of losing your own special rational relationship to the world with which you entered this existence. But you know that this did not first appear at the time of your birth; it existed independently of the birth of your animal self and so cannot be affected by its death.

Why Do Men
Stupefy Themselves?

By 1888, when he was sixty, Tolstoy had renounced
the consumption of meat, alcohol and tobacco. The
following year, he wrote a passionately anti-smoking
and anti-drinking essay called *Why Do Men Stupefy
Themselves?* His answer was that they wanted to blunt
their consciences. If they were sober, they would realize that they were living in the wrong way. Whatever
you think of this argument, it is hard not to believe
Tolstoy when he says that most politicians and educated people in positions of responsibility are under
the influence of alcohol for a substantial part of each
day. It does help to explain why the world is such a
crazy place.

Why Do Men
Stupefy Themselves?

For man is both a spiritual and an animal being. One can move a man either by influencing his animal being or by influencing his spiritual essence. In the same way one can change the time on a clock either by moving the hands or by moving the main wheel. And just as it is better to change the time by moving the inner mechanism, so it is better to move a man – whether oneself or another person – by influencing his consciousness.

And just as one must take special care of the part of the clock which most easily moves the inner mechanism, so one must take special care of the clarity and purity of the consciousness which moves a man. All this is indisputable and everyone knows it; what we must consider, however, is man's need to deceive himself.

What people most want is not that their consciousness should work correctly; it is that their actions should appear to them to be just. It is for this end that they use substances which disturb the correct working of their consciousness.

CHAPTER FIVE

People smoke and drink not out of boredom or in order to cheer themselves up, not simply because they like it, but in order to suppress their conscience. If that is true, then the consequences must be awful indeed. Imagine a building constructed by people who, instead of using a rule and a square to get the walls perpendicular and the corners rectangular, used a soft rule which adapted to the irregularities in the wall and a square which bent to fit any angle, acute or obtuse!

But this is just what happens in life when we intoxicate ourselves. Life does not accord with our conscience, so we bend our conscience to fit life. This happens in the life of individuals, and in the life of humanity as a whole – composed as it is of separate individuals.

In order to grasp the full significance of this clouding of consciousness, let everyone carefully bring to mind the state of their soul at each period of their life. Everyone will find that at each period of his life he was confronted by several moral dilemmas, and that his well-being depended on the correct resolution of these dilemmas. The resolution of such dilemmas requires a degree of attention which constitutes true labour. In any labour, especially at the beginning, there comes a time when the work seems painfully difficult, and our human weakness prompts us to abandon it. Physical labour seems painful at the beginning; intellectual labour all the more so. As Lessing says, people have a tendency to stop thinking when it first becomes difficult; and it is at that point, I would add, that thinking becomes fruitful. A man senses that the resolution of the questions before him demands labour – often painful labour – and he wants to evade this. If he had no means of stupefying himself, he would be unable to drive the questions out of his consciousness, and he would be forced, against his will, to resolve them. Instead of this, however, he has found means to drive the questions away as soon as they arise. As soon as the questions demanding resolution begin to torment him, he resorts to these means and so avoids the anxiety they evoke. His consciousness ceases to demand a resolution, and the unresolved questions remain unresolved until the next moment of clarity. But at this next moment of clarity he does exactly the same; often he remains entire months, years or even his whole life, confronted by the same moral questions, failing to take even one step towards their resolution. And yet it is the resolution of moral questions that constitutes the movement of life.

It is almost as though a man who wanted to see to the bottom of some muddy water in order to lay his hands on a precious pearl, but who wanted not to have to enter the water, were to stir up the water on purpose as soon as it began to settle and clear. Often a man stupefies himself all through his life, staying with the same obscure, self-contradictory view of the world to which he is accustomed, pushing at every moment of dawning clarity against the same wall as he did ten or twenty years before, unable to break through the wall because he has consciously blunted the blade of thought which alone could penetrate it.

Let every man think of himself at a time when he was drinking or smoking, and let everyone do the same with his experience of others, and he will see a constant line distinguishing those who indulge in stupefying substances from those who do not. The more a man stupefies himself, the more fixed he is in his morals.

CHAPTER SIX

The consequences of taking opium or hashish have been described, and they are indeed terrible for certain individuals; we all know only too well the effect of alcohol on confirmed drunkards; but something incomparably more terrible is the consequence for our society as a whole of what is considered the harmless, moderate use of vodka, wine, beer and tobacco, something especially prevalent among the so-called educated classes. These consequences must indeed be terrible if one admits what can hardly be denied: that the direction of society, the political, official, scientific, literary and artistic direction, is provided for the main part by people who are in an abnormal state, that of drunkenness.

It is commonly supposed that someone who, like most members of the well-to-do classes, drinks alcohol with almost every meal, is in a quite normal and sober condition while he is at work the following day. But this is not so. A man who yesterday drank a bottle of wine, a glass of vodka or two mugs of ale, is today in the state of hang-over or depression which usually follows excitement, an intellectually depressed state which is still further aggravated by smoking. Someone who smokes and drinks moderately but regularly needs to spend at least a week without drinking or smoking in order for his brain to return to a normal condition. And this seldom happens.

So it is that most of what is done in our society, whether by those who control and exhort others, or by those who are themselves controlled and exhorted, is carried out by people who are in a condition that is far from sober.

This is not to be taken as a joke or an exaggeration. The horror, and above all the meaninglessness, of our lives is caused primarily by the constant state of intoxication in which most people live. Could sober people calmly perform the actions we see around us – from the construction of the Eiffel Tower to universal conscription?

Without any need whatsoever a company is formed, capital is collected, and people work, calculate and draw up plans. Millions of working days and thousands of tons of iron are expended in order to construct a tower. Millions of people then consider it their duty to climb up this tower, stay on it for a while and climb back down again. And none of this has any effect on people except to make them wish to build still higher towers in other places. Could sober people behave like this?

Take another example. All the peoples of Europe have been busy for decades thinking up the most efficient ways of killing people, and teaching them to all their young men who reach adulthood. Everyone knows that there is no question of a barbarian invasion, that these preparations for murder are directed by civilized Christian peoples against one another. Everyone knows that this is difficult, painful, inconvenient, wasteful, impious and insane – and yet they continue to prepare to murder one another. Some are involved in political scheming as to who is in alliance with whom in order to kill whom; some preside over those who are preparing to commit murder; others submit to these preparations against their own will, conscience and reason. Could sober people behave like this? Only drunk-ards, drunkards who never sober up, could do these things and continue to suffer the appalling conflict between life and conscience in which everyone in our society is caught, not only in this, but also in all other respects.

Never, I believe, have people suffered such an obvious conflict between the actions they perform and the demands made on them by their consciences.

It is as though humanity today has got stuck against something, as though there were some external factor holding it back from the state which is natural to its consciousness. And this factor – the main, if not the only, reason – is the physical stupefaction that most people in our society bring on themselves through their use of alcohol and tobacco.

A deliverance from this terrible evil will mark a new epoch in the life of humanity, and I believe this epoch is about to set in. The evil has been recognized. A change of consciousness with regard to the use of intoxicating substances has already occurred. People understand the terrible harm they occasion, and are beginning to point it out; and this almost unnoticed change in perception is certain to bring about a general deliverance.

A deliverance from intoxicating substances will open people's eyes to the demand of their consciousness, and they will then begin to live their lives in accord with conscience. I think this is already beginning. But, as always, it is beginning among the upper classes only after all the lower classes have been infected.

An Afterword To
'The Kreutzer Sonata'

Though able to give up alcohol and tobacco, Tolstoy
was never really able to give up sex – a fact which
tormented him. In 1889, he finished a story called *The
Kreutzer Sonata* in which a lunatic murders his wife in a
fit of sexual jealousy. In the course of relating this
crime, the lunatic comes to expound the view that
sexual love, especially in marriage, was positively
harmful. Only a few years before in *What I Believe*
(1883) Tolstoy had commended the virtue and necessity of sexual relations within marriage. He had
changed his mind partly as a result of reading tracts,
posted to him by an American sect called the Shakers,
who advocate total celibacy at all times and who, not
surprisingly, have therefore dwindled almost to
extinction in our own times. Tolstoy's wife, who had
just given birth to her thirteenth baby, and who was
having to take the greatest precautions to avoid con-
ceiving a fourteenth before the wide-spread publica-
tion of this notorious story, took a dim view of it all.
But when the story was banned by the censor, she
bravely went in person to remonstrate with the
Emperor and persuaded him (Alexander III) to allow
the story to be reprinted in the Collected Edition of
Tolstoy's works. The story itself, and the actions of his
wife, caused wide-spread questions to be asked.
What? Never? It was in order to answer these questions about sexual morality that Tolstoy wrote his
Afterword to 'The Kreutzer Sonata'. The views which it
expresses about sex, and about women, are unlikely to
win much acceptance today. What is interesting, is

how authentically Christian they are. As in the case of pacifism, Tolstoy has the New Testament and the Early Church on his side. So often his religious writings have the rather Voltairean effect upon us of making us dismiss as Tolstoyan crankiness what is in fact hard core Christian ethical teaching.

An Afterword To 'The Kreutzer Sonata'

I have received, and am still continuing to receive, many letters from strangers asking me to explain clearly and simply what I mean by my story, *The Kreutzer Sonata*. I shall try to do this, to express as simply as possible the essence of what I wanted to say in this story and the conclusions I believe can be drawn from it.

First of all I wanted to say that a strong belief, supported by a false science, has taken root in all classes of our society, a belief that sexual intercourse is indispensable to health; since marriage is not always possible, sexual intercourse outside marriage, with the man incurring no obligation other than a monetary payment, is considered to be something entirely natural and so to be encouraged. This belief has now become so widely held and firmly established that parents arrange debauchery for their children on doctors' orders; governments – whose only concern should be the moral well-being of their citizens – also organize debauchery, regulating the lives of a whole class of women who are obliged to perish, both physically and spiritually, in order to satisfy the supposed needs of men; the unmarried, meanwhile, give themselves up to debauchery with an untroubled conscience.

And what I wanted to say is that this is wrong; it cannot be true that some people need to be destroyed, body and soul, for the health of others. This could no more be true than that some people, for reasons of health, need to drink the blood of others.

The natural conclusion to be drawn from this is that we should not yield to this error and deception. In order to do this, we must first of all refuse to believe in immoral teachings, whatever the false sciences that uphold them. Secondly, we must understand that for a man to enter into sexual intercourse and either abandon the children that are a possible consequence, or lay all the responsibility for them on the woman, or prevent the possibility of their being born, is a shameful violation of the most basic claims of morality. An unmarried person who does not wish to act shamefully should not do this.

In order for people to abstain, they must lead a natural way of life. They must not drink, eat flesh, or over-eat; they must not avoid labour – not play or gymnastics, but real, exhausting labour; they must not allow, even in thought, the possibility of intercourse with other women – any more than they would conceive of such a thing with their own mothers, sisters, relatives or the friends of their wives.

Any man can find hundreds of proofs round about him that such restraint is not only possible, but also less dangerous and injurious to health than its opposite.

That is the first thing I wanted to say.

The second is that we look on sexual intercourse not only as a pleasure and a necessary precondition for health, but also as a poetic and exalted blessing. As a result, conjugal infidelity has become commonplace in all classes of our society. (Among the peasants this is due chiefly to conscription.)

I consider this to be wrong. And my conclusion is that people should not behave in this way.

In order for this to happen, our view of sexual love must be changed. Men and women must be taught, both by their own families and by public opinion, to look on falling-in-love and the accompanying sexual desire – whether before or after marriage – not as something poetic and exalted, but as an animal-like state that is degrading to a human being. A violation of the promise of fidelity given in marriage, instead of being praised in novels, poems, songs and operas, should be punished by society at least as seriously as business fraud or a failure to pay debts.

That is the second thing I wanted to say.

The third is that, as a result of this false importance attached to sexual love, childbirth in our society has lost its meaning. Instead of being the aim and justification of marriage, it is seen as a hindrance to the pleasure of continued sexual relations. As a result, advised by their doctors, both the married and the unmarried have begun to use means to prevent the birth of children. At the same time a practice has become common which was never heard of previously and still is unheard of in patriarchal peasant families: the continuation of conjugal relations while the woman is pregnant or nursing.

I consider this to be wrong. It is wrong to use means to prevent childbirth; firstly because it releases men and women from concern for their children and the many tasks which serve to redeem sexual love, secondly because it is very close indeed to murder, the act which is most shocking of all to our consciences. As for incontinence while the woman is pregnant or nursing, that is wrong because it exhausts the woman's physical, and more importantly her spiritual, strength.

And the conclusion to be drawn is that this should not be done. It is essential that we understand that abstinence, something indispensable to the dignity of the unmarried, is still more important to the married.

That is the third point.

The fourth is that in our society, where children are seen either as an obstacle to pleasure, an unfortunate accident, or – if only a prearranged number are born – as a kind of pleasure in themselves, their upbringing is determined not by the nature of the tasks that await them as creatures capable of reason and love, but only by the possible gratification they may afford the parents. As a result, these children are brought up like the young of animals; the main concern of the parents, a concern encouraged by a false medical science, is not to prepare them for activities worthy of human beings, but to feed them as well as possible and make them grow quickly, to have them clean, white, well-fed and good-looking. (If the lower classes fail to do this, it is simply because they are unable to; their views are precisely the same.) And these pampered children, like any other over-fed animals, develop an overpowering sensuousness at an unnaturally young age which occasions them great suffering as adolescents. Their whole environment, their clothes, their books, their music, their dances, their sweet food – everything from the pictures on boxes to novels, stories and poems – joins together to further inflame this sensuousness. As a result, the most terrible sexual vices and illnesses are only too common among children of either sex, often persisting even when they are adult.

And I consider this to be wrong. The conclusion to be drawn is that we should stop bringing up our children like the young of animals. We should set ourselves other goals in bringing up human children than producing a handsome and sleek body.

That is the fourth point.

The fifth is that in our society, where love between a young man and woman, based on physical attraction, is extolled by the whole of our art and poetry as the highest and most poetic aim of human endeavour, young people spend the best years of their lives in the following way: the men devote themselves to seeking out, pursuing and possessing – whether through marriage or a free liaison – the most desirable objects of love; while the girls and young women devote themselves to luring and entrapping men into marriage or a liaison.

And so people waste the best of their powers in activities that are not only unproductive, but even harmful. This is the origin of most of the insane luxury of our way of life, of the idleness of men and the shamelessness of women who, following fashions borrowed from the depraved, are not above exposing those parts of the body that most excite sensuality.

And I consider this to be wrong.

It is wrong because, however it may be idealized, the aim of coupling with the object of one's love is an aim as unworthy of a man as that of obtaining plentiful and tasty food – though this too is seen by many as the highest of goods.

The conclusion to be drawn from this is that we must cease thinking of sexual love as something especially exalted. We must understand that no aim worthy of a man, whether it be the service of humanity, of the fatherland, of Science or Art – let alone that of God – can be attained by means of coupling with the object of one's love, whether within or outside marriage. On the contrary, for all the attempts in prose or verse to prove the contrary, falling in love and sexual intercourse invariably make it more difficult for a man to achieve any worthwhile goal.

That is the fifth point.

That is the essence of what I wanted to say, what I thought I had said, in my story. I had thought that there was room for discussion about how best to remedy the evils I had pointed out, but that it would be impossible not to agree with my general thesis. In the first place my thesis was fully in accord not only with the progress of humanity, which has always advanced from depravity towards an ever-increasing purity, but also with the moral understanding of society and the dictates of our own conscience, which has always condemned depravity and valued purity. In the second place, my thesis was nothing more than an inevitable conclusion from the teachings of the gospels, which we all either openly profess or, at the very least, unconsciously acknowledge as the basis of our conception of morality.

I was, however, mistaken. No one, admittedly, has contested the principle that one should not behave in a depraved manner either before or after marriage, that one should not use artificial means to prevent childbirth, that children should not be made into mere playthings, and that we should not attach a supreme value to sexual coupling; no one, in short, questions that purity is better than depravity. But what they do say is this: 'If celibacy is better than marriage, then it is clear that people should do what is best. But if they do what is best, then the human race will come to an end – and humanity's ideal cannot be its own destruction.'

Leaving aside the fact that the idea of humanity's destruction is nothing new, that to the religious it is an article of faith, while to the scientific it is an inescapable conclusion from observations of the cooling of the sun, we find in this objection an important, wide-spread and long-held misunderstanding. The argument runs: 'If people should attain the ideal of absolute chastity, they would become extinct; it follows that the ideal is false.' This, however, is an intentional or unintentional confusion of two different orders of things: a rule or precept and an ideal.

Chastity is not a rule or precept; it is an ideal, or rather, one condition of the ideal. But an ideal can only be an ideal if its realization is possible only ideally, only in thought, if it is attainable only in infinity and the possibilities for drawing closer to it are therefore infinite. If an ideal could be attained, if we could even imagine it being attained, it would cease to be an ideal. Such is the ideal of Christ – the establishment on Earth of the Kingdom of God, an ideal foretold by the prophets of a time when all people are taught by God, when they beat their swords into plough-shares and their spears into pruning-hooks, when the lion lies down with the lamb and all creatures are united by love. The whole meaning of human life lies in progress towards this ideal. It follows that the aspiration towards the Christian ideal in its entirety, and towards chastity as one of the conditions of this ideal, does not in any way exclude the possibility of life. On the contrary, the absence of the Christian ideal would destroy the possibility of progress, and with it the possibility of life.

The argument that the human race would come to an end if people strove with all their powers towards chastity is like the possible argument – sometimes actually put forward – that the human race would perish if people, instead of struggling for survival, strove with all their powers to love everything living, their enemies as well as their friends. These arguments are engendered by a failure to distinguish between two kinds of moral guidance.

Just as there are two methods for showing the way to a traveller, so there are two methods for giving moral guidance to someone searching for truth. The first is to tell a man what landmarks he will meet on the road; he will then be able to orientate himself on them. The second is simply to give a man a bearing on a compass that he carries with him; on it he will be able to make out one unchanging direction and every deviation from it.

The first method of moral guidance is through external rules: a man is simply told which acts he should carry out, and which he should not carry out. 'Observe the Sabbath'; 'Have yourself circumcized'; 'Do not steal'; 'Do not drink anything intoxicating'; 'Do not kill anything living'; 'Give tithes to the poor'; 'Do not commit adultery'; 'Wash and pray five times a day'; 'Make the sign of the Cross'; 'Receive the Eucharist'; and so on. These are the decrees of external religious teachings: Brahmin, Buddhist, Muhammadan, Jewish, and the ecclesiastical teaching falsely referred to as Christian.

The second method is that of pointing out to a man an unattainable perfection, a striving towards which he will recognize within himself. Knowing the ideal, he is able to detect any deviation from it.

'Love the Lord thy God with all thy heart, and with all thy soul . . . and with all thy mind; and love thy neighbour as thyself. . . . Be ye perfect, just as your Father in Heaven is perfect' (Luke 10:27 and Matthew 5:48).

Such is the teaching of Christ.

The test of observance of external religious teachings is whether or not our conduct conforms with their decrees. Such conformity is indeed possible.

The test of observance of Christ's teachings is our consciousness of our failure to attain an ideal perfection. The degree to which we draw near this perfection cannot be seen; all we can see is the extent of our deviation.

A man who professes an external law is like someone standing in the light of a lantern fixed to a post. It is light all round him, but there is nowhere further for him to walk. A man who professes the teaching of Christ is like a man carrying a lantern before him on a long, or not so long, pole: the light is in front of him, always lighting up fresh ground and always encouraging him to walk further.

The Pharisee thanks God that he himself fulfils the whole of the law. The rich young man has also fulfilled the whole of the law since childhood, and is unable to understand what can be lacking. And it is impossible for either of them to think otherwise: there is nothing ahead of them to which they could aspire. Tithes have been paid, Sabbaths observed, parents honoured, they have not committed robbery, adultery or murder. What else is there? For anyone who follows the Christian teaching the attainment of any degree of perfection evokes the need to reach a higher degree, from which can be seen a still higher degree, and so on without end.

A man who follows the law of Christ is always in the position of the publican. He always feels himself to be imperfect, unaware of the path he has travelled, aware only of the path ahead he has yet to travel.

This is the difference between the teaching of Christ and that of all other religions, a difference not in the demands made but in the nature of the guidance afforded. Christ never laid down rules of conduct. He established no institutions, not even that of marriage. But people who failed to understand the uniqueness of Christ's teachings, who were accustomed to external laws and who wished, like the Pharisee, to feel themselves justified – these people constructed from the letter of Christ's teaching, contrary to its whole spirit, a set of external laws called the teaching of the Christian Church. And this teaching has supplanted the true Christian teaching of the ideal.

The so-called Christian teachings of the Church have replaced Christ's teaching of the ideal, with external rules and regulations contrary to the whole spirit of His teaching. This has been done with regard to government, law and war, with regard to the Church and with regard to worship. It has been done with regard to marriage: in spite of the fact that Christ not only never instituted marriage but (if we must seek external regulations) appeared rather to disapprove of it ('Leave your wife and follow me') – in spite of this the Church has established marriage as a Christian institution. That is to say, it has laid down external conditions under which sexual love is apparently quite right and legitimate for a Christian.

But, since there are no foundations in Christian teaching for the institution of marriage, what has happened is that people in our society have left one shore and not yet arrived at the other. Sensing the lack of foundation for this institution, they do not truly believe in the Church's definitions of marriage. At the same time, since it is obscured by the teachings of the Church, they are unable to see ahead of them the ideal of Christ, the aspiration towards absolute chastity. As a result, they are left without any guidance at all with regard to marriage. This is the reason for the apparently strange fact that conjugal fidelity and the principle of the family are considerably less strong among so-called Christians than among Jews, Muhammadans, Lamaists and many others who follow religious teachings, considerably inferior to those of Christianity, which lay down definite external regulations with regard to marriage.

These other religions allow concubinage and polygamy within clearly defined limits. We, on the other hand, allow total depravity: concubinage, polygamy and polyandry concealed by a pretence of monogamy and unbounded by any regulations whatsoever.

For the simple reason that the clergy are paid to perform a ceremony known as a wedding service over a certain proportion of couples who come together – for this reason alone people naïvely or hypocritically imagine that ours is a monogamous society.

There never has been and never can be such a thing as a Christian marriage – just as there never has been and never can be Christian worship, Christian teachers or Church Fathers, Christian property, or Christian armies, law courts and governments. All this was clearly understood by the true Christians of the first centuries.

The Christian ideal is love for God and one's neighbour, together with self-renunciation in order to serve God and one's neighbour. Sexual love and marriage are a service of self, and so at the very least an obstacle to the service of God and other people; from a Christian point of view they are a falling away, a sin.

The act of marriage cannot be a way of serving God and one's fellow men even if one enters into it with the aim of perpetuating the human race. It would be simpler, rather than getting married in order to engender more lives, to save and support the millions of children who perish round about us for want of food for their bodies, let alone food for their souls.

A Christian could only get married without a sense of fall, of sin, if he knew that every child alive was adequately provided for.

One can refuse to accept Christ's teaching, a teaching that permeates all our life and is the basis for our morality. If, however, one does accept it, then one cannot deny that it points to absolute chastity as an ideal.

The gospels clearly state, allowing no possibility of any other interpretation: firstly, that a man should not divorce his wife in order to take another woman; secondly, that it is sinful for a man, whether married or unmarried, to look on a woman as an object of pleasure; thirdly, that it is better for an unmarried man not to marry at all, to remain entirely chaste.

To many people these thoughts seem strange and even contradictory. They are indeed contradictory; and they contradict not one another, but our whole life. The doubt inevitably arises: which is right – these thoughts or my own life and that of millions of others?

I, too, experienced this same feeling very strongly indeed as I approached the conclusions I am now stating; I never expected the development of my thoughts to lead me to where it has done. I was appalled at my own conclusions; I wished not to believe them, but found it impossible. However they contradicted our whole way of life, however they contradicted what I had thought and said previously, I had to accept them.

'But though they may be true, all these are just general considerations. They relate to the teaching of Christ and are binding on those who follow it. But life is life and it is impossible merely to point ahead to an unattainable ideal and then leave men with no other guidance in the face of one of the most universal and distressing of problems. A young and passionate man will at first be attracted by this ideal, but he will not be able to endure. Instead he will break down and, neither knowing nor acknowledging any rules, will fall into utter depravity.'

These are the usual objections. 'The Christian ideal is unattainable and so cannot be of guidance in real life. One can think and dream about it, but it is not applicable to life itself and must therefore be abandoned. What we need is not an ideal but a rule, a means of guidance suited to our own capacities, to the moral average of our society: a proper church marriage, or a not so proper marriage in which one party – the man – has already known many other women, or a marriage with the possibility of divorce, or a civil marriage, or even – going a little further – a Japanese-style marriage for a limited period of time. Or even brothels. Why not?'

Brothels are indeed said to be preferable to prostitution on the streets.

And that is the problem. Once we allow ourselves to adapt the ideal to our own weakness, it is impossible to define a boundary at which we must stop.

This whole line of reasoning is fundamentally unsound. It is not true that the ideal of infinite perfection cannot be a means of guidance in life and that we must either throw it away, saying that since it is unattainable it is also useless, or else lower it to a level that is adapted to our own weakness.

It is as though a sailor were to say: 'Since I cannot keep to the bearing indicated by my compass, then I must either stop looking at the compass or even throw it out (i.e. abandon the ideal), or else fasten the compass needle so that it points out the direction in which my ship is travelling at the given moment (i.e. adapt the ideal to my own weakness).' Christ's ideal of perfection is neither a dream nor a rhetorical exhortation; it is the most indispensable and generally accessible form of guidance for our moral life – just as the compass is the most indispensable and accessible instrument of guidance for a sailor. All that is required is to believe in the former as strongly as in the latter.

Whatever situation a man may encounter, Christ's teaching of the ideal is always enough to show him what he should or should not do. But he must fully believe in the teaching and in the teaching alone. He must cease to believe in any others – just as a sailor must believe in the compass alone and not be guided by what he sees around him.

One must learn to be guided by Christian teaching, just as one must study a compass; the main thing is to understand one's situation and not be afraid to define precisely one's deviation from the ideal direction. Whatever position a man may have reached, it is always possible for him to draw closer to the ideal; he can never say that he has already attained it and cannot aspire further. All this applies to the nature of man's aspiration to the Christian ideal in general and to the ideal of chastity in particular. Christ's teaching affords a clear and definite guidance as to what a man should or should not do at every stage of his life – from the innocence of childhood to the condition of marriage without restraint.

What should a pure young man do, or a pure young woman? They should keep themselves free from temptation and – so as to be able to give all their strength to the service of God and other people – they should aspire to an ever-increasing purity of thought and desire.

What should a young man or woman do if they have fallen into temptation, if they have been swallowed up by thoughts of abstract love or of love for a particular person, and have therefore to some degree lost the ability to serve God and other people? They should do the same; they should not allow themselves to fall; they should remember that, far from releasing them from temptation, a fall will only increase the power of further temptation. And they should aspire to an ever-increasing chastity, so they can more fully serve both God and other people.

What should people do if they have been defeated by the struggle, if they have fallen? They should look on their fall neither as legitimate enjoyment, sanctioned by the rite of marriage, nor as a casual pleasure to be repeated with others, nor, if they have been with an inferior and with no preceding church ritual, as a disaster. Instead they should look on this first fall as their only fall, as the beginning of an indissoluble marriage.

Through the children that are its consequence, this marriage restricts the man and woman to a new, more limited form of service to God and other people. Before marriage they could be of direct service to God and other people in the most varied ways; marriage limits their possible activities, requiring that they should rear and feed the children who will be of service to God in the future.

What should a man and woman do if they are married, if they are rearing and feeding their children, serving God in the limited way that is appropriate to their position?

They should do the same. They should aspire together to free themselves from temptation, to purify themselves and to refrain from sin. They should strive to substitute the pure relationship of a brother and sister for the physical love that hinders them from serving God and other people.

It is not true that Christ's ideal is too lofty, too perfect and unattainable for us to use it as a means of guidance. We are unable to use it as a means of guidance simply because we lie to ourselves.

We may say we need rules that are more easily realized, that otherwise, falling short of Christ's ideal, we shall lapse into depravity, but what we really mean is that we do not believe in this ideal and do not wish to regulate our lives according to it. To say that any fall will lead us into depravity is to say that we have decided in advance that a fall with an inferior is not a sin but a distraction or amusement that we are not bound to set right by what we call marriage. If we understood that any fall is a sin that can only be redeemed – and must be redeemed – by an indissoluble marriage and all the activities surrounding the rearing of children, then a fall could never bring about a lapse into depravity.

It is as though a peasant only considered a field sown if the sowing had been successful, as though he went on to sow a second and third field and only attended to the field he had sown successfully. He would obviously waste a great deal of land and seed and never learn to sow. But take chastity as your ideal, consider any fall whatsoever as a unique and indissoluble marriage – and it will become clear that Christ's guidance is not only adequate but the only guidance that is possible.

'Man is weak, you must set him a task within his powers', people say. That is like saying, 'My hands are weak and I cannot draw a straight line. In order to make things easier, I shall take a crooked or broken line as a model.' The weaker my hand, the greater my need of a perfect model.

Once we have known the Christian teaching of the ideal, it is impossible to act as though we did not know it and replace it by external regulations. The Christian teaching of the ideal has been given to us because it is best suited to guide us in our present state. Humanity has grown out of the period of external religious regulations and we no longer believe in them.

The Christian teaching of the ideal is the only teaching which can serve to guide humanity. It is both wrong and impossible to replace Christ's ideal by external rules; we must keep this ideal clearly before us in all its purity. Above all, we must believe in it.

While a sailor keeps near the coast, one can say: 'Steer by that cliff, that cape, that tower.'

But there comes a time when the sailors are far from the shore and the only possible guidance is from the unattainable heavenly luminaries and the compass indicating a direction.

Both of these have been given to us.

The Kingdom of God Is Within You (1)

The Kingdom of God Is Within You was finished by 1894, but was the fruit of many years' reading, writing, and meditating on what Tolstoy took to be the authentic teaching of Christ. In this passage, he reiterates the idea that Christ taught us five basic commandments. If we followed these ideals we would be perfect. But Christ knew, as all wise men have known, that we are not perfect. It is precisely for that reason that we should strive after ideals.

The Kingdom of God Is Within You (1)

Christ is teaching not angels, but people who live an animal life and are motivated by it. To this animal motive force Christ has added the new motive force of the consciousness of divine perfection, thus directing the movement of life along the resultant of these two forces.

To suppose that human life will follow the direction indicated by Christ is like supposing that a ferryman, pointing his boat almost directly against the current in order to cross a swift river, will actually move in that direction.

Christ recognizes the existence of both sides of the parallelogram, of both the eternal and indestructible forces that compose man's life: the force of his animal nature, and the force of his consciousness of being the son of God. Christ says nothing of the animal force – which always asserts itself, always remains the same and is beyond man's power – and speaks only of the divine force, calling man to recognize it as fully as possible, to free it as completely as possible from all that holds it back, and to bring it to the highest degree of intensity.

It is this liberation and intensification of the divine force that, according to the teaching of Christ, constitutes man's true life. Earlier conventions held true life to lie in the execution of the law; Christ's teaching holds it to lie in the nearest possible approach to a divine perfection that has been shown to man and that he can recognize within himself, in drawing ever closer to a fusion of one's own will with God's will, a fusion towards which man strives and which would mark the destruction of life as we know it.

Human life is like a hyperbola, always striving towards a

divine perfection that it is able to attain only in infinity.

The Christian teaching appears to make life impossible only if you mistake the indication of an ideal for the laying down of a rule. It is only then that the demands made by the Christian teaching appear to be destructive of life. In reality it is these teachings alone that allow the possibility of a true life.

'It's no good asking too much', people usually say as they discuss the demands made by the Christian teaching. 'It is impossible to demand, in the words of the Gospel, that we should take no care for the future – though it is indeed wrong to be over-concerned about it. It is impossible to give everything to the poor – though one should give them a certain, pre-determined portion. It is wrong to aspire to chastity – though one should indeed avoid vice. It is wrong to abandon one's wife and children – though one should indeed avoid too strong a predilection for them.'

All this is like telling the ferryman, as he points his boat against the current of a swift river, that it is impossible to cross the river like that, that he should point his boat in the direction in which he wishes to travel.

Christ's teaching differs from earlier teachings in that it guides people not through external rules, but through an inner consciousness of the possibility of reaching divine perfection. And what we find in man's soul is not measured rules about justice and philanthropy, but the ideal of complete, infinite divine perfection. Only the aspiration towards this perfection is enough to take the direction of man's life away from the animal condition and – as far as is possible in this life – towards the divine condition.

In order to reach one's goal, one must strive with all one's strength towards something much higher.

To lower the demands of the ideal means not only to diminish the possibility of perfection but to destroy the ideal itself. What acts on people is not an invented ideal, but the ideal that every man carries within his own soul. Only the ideal of absolute perfection can influence people and motivate them to action. Moderate perfection has no power to act on men's souls.

Christ's teaching only has power when it demands absolute perfection, that is the fusion of the divine essence in every man's soul with the will of God, the union of the son and the father. It is only this liberation of the divine son from the animal, its reconciliation with the father, that according to Christ's teaching constitutes true life.

The existence within man of the animal, of the animal alone, is not human life. Nor can life entirely in accord with God's will be called human life. Human life is a compound of animal and divine life. And the nearer this compound approaches the divine, the more life there is.

According to the Christian teaching, life is a movement towards divine perfection. There is therefore no condition that is higher or lower than any other condition. Every condition is only a particular stage, of no merit within itself, on the road towards an unattainable perfection. The only true increase of life, according to the teaching, is in the quickening of the movement towards perfection. This is why the movement towards perfection of Zacchaeus the publican, of the prostitute, of the thief on the cross, constitutes a higher degree of perfection than the unchanging righteousness of the Pharisee. This is why the teaching cannot contain obligatory rules. A man on the very lowest step, but who is moving towards perfection, is living better, more morally, more in accordance with the teaching than someone morally considerably more advanced who is not moving towards perfection.

It is in this sense that the lost sheep is dearer to the father than the ones that have not strayed. The Prodigal Son, and the coin that has been lost and found again, are more precious than those that were never lost.

The fulfilment of the teaching lies in the movement from oneself towards God. It is obvious that for this there can be no definite rules or laws. All degrees of perfection, and all degrees of imperfection, are equal in the light of this teaching; no mere fulfilment of laws can constitute a fulfilment of the teaching; it is for this reason that there are no – and never can be any – obligatory rules or laws.

It is this radical difference between Christ's teaching and all preceding teachings – founded as they are on a social understanding of life – that gives rise to the difference between the Christian and the social commandments. The social commandments are for the main part positive, prescribing certain actions which justify people and make them righteous. The Christian commandments (the commandment of love is not, strictly speaking, a commandment, but rather a distillation of the teaching), the five commandments of the Sermon on the Mount are all negative; they only show what, at a certain stage of humanity's progress, men no longer need to do. They are like signs on the never-ending road along which we are travelling; what they indicate is the degree of perfection possible at a particular stage of humanity's progress.

In the Sermon on the Mount Christ expressed both the eternal ideal towards which it is natural for us to aspire, and the degree to which it is now possible for us to attain it.

The ideal is not to harbour ill-will against anyone, not to provoke ill-will, and to love everyone; the precept, indicating a level it is quite possible for us to keep to in our pursuit of the ideal, is not to offend anyone in word. This is the first commandment.

The ideal is absolute chastity, even in thought; the precept, indicating a level it is quite possible for us to keep to in our pursuit of the ideal, is that of a pure married life free from adultery. This is the second commandment.

The ideal is to take no thought for the future, to live in the present; the precept, indicating a level it is quite possible for us to keep to, is not to swear oaths and not to make promises for the future. This is the third commandment.

The ideal is not to use violence in the pursuit of any aim whatsoever; the precept, indicating a level it is quite possible for us to keep to, is not to repay evil with evil, to endure insults and to give up one's shirt. This is the fourth commandment.

The ideal is to love our enemies and those that hate us; the precept, indicating a level it is quite possible for us to keep to, is to do no harm to our enemies, to speak well of them and not to make distinctions between them and our fellow citizens. This is the fifth commandment.

All these commandments are indications of what we are now quite capable of avoiding, what we need to work towards and transform into unconscious habits. But far from exhausting the teaching, these precepts merely constitute one of the innumerable steps on the path towards perfection. Beyond them must and will follow other commandments that are still loftier.

It is therefore in the nature of Christianity to make greater demands than those expressed in these commandments; it is certainly not in its nature to lower the demands either of the ideal itself or of the commandments – as is often done by people judging Christianity from the point of view of social understanding.

I have discussed one misunderstanding held by scientific people with regard to the significance of Christ's teaching; another, springing from the same source, is to substitute the love and service of humanity for the love and service of God.

The Christian teaching that we must love and serve God, that the love and service of our neighbour is merely a consequence of this, appears to scientific people to be obscure, mystical and arbitrary. They entirely reject the love and service of God, considering the love and service of humanity to be more comprehensible, more real and more valid.

Scientific people teach in theory that the only good and reasonable life is a life of service to humanity; they consider this to be the import – the whole import – of the Christian teaching. They look in the Christian teaching for confirmation of this teaching of their own, believing the two teachings to be one and the same.

This opinion is entirely mistaken. The Christian teaching and the teaching of the Communists, Positivists and other propagandists of a universal brotherhood of man, based on the practical benefits of such a brotherhood, have nothing whatsoever in common. One especially important difference is that the Christian teaching has a clear and solid foundation in the human soul, whereas the teaching of love for humanity is merely a theoretical deduction by analogy.

The doctrine of love for humanity alone is based on a social understanding of life.

The essence of the social understanding of life lies in the handing over of the meaning of one's own life to the life of a group of individuals: a family, a tribe, a race or a State. In its first stages – the transference of the meaning of life to the family or tribe – this process is easy and natural. The transference of the meaning of life to the nation or people is more difficult and requires special training. To transfer this consciousness to the State is the limit of which we are capable.

It is natural to love oneself, and everyone does this without any special encouragement. It is also natural to love the tribe that supports and defends me, the wife who is my joy and help, the children who are my hope and consolation, and the parents who have given me my life and reared me. This kind of love, though not so strong as love of oneself, is common enough.

A love of race or nation for one's own sake, out of personal pride, is less common but still to be met with. A love for one's own people, who are of the same blood, who speak the same language and who hold the same faith, is still possible – though it is a feeling of considerably less power than love for one's tribe or family, let alone love of oneself. Love of a State, however – love of Turkey, Germany, England, Austria or Russia – is something almost impossible, something that in spite of intensified propaganda does not really exist but is only assumed to exist. It is at this point that man's ability to transfer his consciousness reaches its limit; he is unable to experience any immediate feelings towards such a fiction as a State.

Positivists and other propagandists of scientific brotherhood, failing to take into account that the feeling grows weaker as its object expands, take this line of reasoning even further. 'If', they say, 'it is of benefit to the individual to transfer his consciousness to the tribe, the family, the people or the State, then it will be of even more benefit if he transfers his consciousness to humanity as a whole. Just as people now live for their family or their State, people in future will live for humanity.'

In theory all this is right. In order for us to escape the conflicts and disasters attendant upon the division of humanity into nations and states, it would indeed be quite logical for us to transfer our love to humanity as a whole. What propagandists of this doctrine fail to notice, however, is that love is a feeling which can be experienced but cannot be artificially inculcated. They also fail to notice that love needs an object, and that humanity is not an object but a fiction.

The tribe, the family and even the State were not invented by human beings; they formed organically, just like a swarm of bees or ants, and they have a real existence. A man, who for the sake of his own animal being loves his family, knows whom he loves: Anna, Marya, Ivan, Peter and so on. A man who loves his kindred and is proud of them knows that he loves all Guelphs and all Ghibellines. A man who loves his State knows that he loves France as far as the Rhine and the Pyrenees, that he loves her capital, Paris, her history and so on. But what does a man love if he loves humanity? There is such a thing as a State or a people. There is indeed such an abstract concept as humanity, but this is not and never can be a concrete reality.

Humanity? What are its limits? Where does it begin and end? Does it include the savage, the idiot, the alcoholic and the madman? If we draw a line through humanity so as to exclude the lowest representatives of the human race, then where shall we draw that line? Shall we follow the Americans in excluding Negroes? Shall we follow certain Englishmen who exclude Indians? Shall we exclude Jews? If we include everyone without exception, then why should we include only people and not the higher animals, many of whom are on a higher level than the lowest representatives of the human race?

We do not know such a thing as humanity, and we do not know its limits. Humanity is a fiction and it is impossible to love it. It would indeed be extremely advantageous if people were able to love humanity in the same way as they love their family. It would indeed be extremely advantageous if, as the Communists recommend, we could organize human activity cooperatively and universally rather than through individualist competition, if each could work for all and all for each – but there is no motivation for this. Positivists, Communists and other propagandists of scientific brotherhood exhort people to extend the love they feel for themselves, their families and their State into love for humanity as a whole. What they forget is that this love of theirs is a personal love, a love which can expand, in a diluted form, into a love of one's family or even, still more diluted, into a love of one's homeland, but which entirely disappears when it is extended to an artificial State such as the Austrian, British or Turkish Empires. And we cannot, of course, even conceive of such a love extended to the entirely mystical conception of humanity as a whole.

'A man loves himself (his animal being). He loves his family, even his homeland. Why should he not also love humanity? It would be so good if he did. And, by the way, Christianity preaches exactly the same thing.' So argue the champions of Positivist, Socialist and Communist brotherhood. And it would indeed be very good; but it is quite impossible, since a love that is founded on a personal and social understanding of life cannot extend beyond love for the State. The mistake in their reasoning is that the social understanding of life is founded on love for oneself, a love that grows continually weaker as it is transferred to family, kindred and nation, reaching its absolute limit when it is transferred to the State.

The need to extend the province of love is indisputable; but this very need destroys the possibility of love and proves the inadequacy of a personal, human love.

It is at this point that the champions of Positivist, Communist or Socialist brotherhood call upon Christian love to buttress this inadequate human love, but they look not to its foundations but only to its effects. What they propose is love for humanity alone, without love for God.

And such a love cannot exist. There is no motivation for it. Christian love can spring only from a Christian understanding of life, an understanding where the meaning of life lies in the love and service of God.

The Kingdom of
God Is Within You (2)

'We are all brothers, yet every morning a brother or a sister carries out my chamber-pot.' The more he meditated upon the matter, and the more he read of the world and its doings, the more certain Tolstoy became that it could only be put right by a return to simple Christian values. The existence of economic differences between the rich and the poor, the oppression of one class by another, the exploitation of labour and men for the purposes of acts of aggression against their fellow human beings, whether as 'police' or soldiers, all struck Tolstoy as incompatible with Christianity. And yet it was those who insisted on their Orthodox or Anglican or Catholic view of Christianity who appeared to be exploiting the poor, fighting wars and preserving societies which depended, for their very existence, on oppression.

The Kingdom of
God Is Within You (2)

The worker of our day, even though his work may be a great
deal easier than that of a slave of antiquity, even though he may
receive three dollars for an eight-hour day, does not suffer any
the less because of this. He works not of his own accord but out
of need, producing things he will never enjoy in order to satisfy
the whims of people who live in idle luxury and, more particularly, in order to create profits for the one wealthy man who
owns the factory. At the same time he is aware that all this is
taking place in a world where not only has it been scientifically
stated that labour alone is wealth and that the exploitation of
other people's labour is unjust and punishable by law, but
where the Christian teaching is professed according to which
we are all brothers, and the worth and dignity of a man lies in
service to his neighbour, not in exploiting him.

He knows all this and cannot but suffer torment from the
glaring contradiction between what is and what should be.
'According to all the facts and what I know people to profess,'
the worker says to himself, 'I should be free, equal to all others
and an object of love, but in reality I am a slave, humiliated and
hated.' And so he himself begins to hate, to look for ways to
deliver himself from his position, ways to shake off the enemy
who is oppressing him, and himself become the oppressor.
People say: 'The workers are wrong to wish to usurp the place
of the capitalists, it is wrong for the poor to sit in the place of the
rich.' This is not so. The workers and the poor would indeed be
wrong if they lived in a world where it was accepted that
masters and slaves, rich and poor, were appointed so by God –
but they live in a world that professes the teaching of the

gospels, a teaching whose first principle is that Man is the son of God and that all men are therefore equal to one another in brotherhood. And however people may try, it cannot be denied that one of the first principles of a Christian life is love, not in words but in deed.

A man belonging to the supposedly educated classes lives in a still greater degree of contradiction and suffering. If such a man believes in anything at all, then he believes at least in humanitarianism if not in the brotherhood of men, in justice if not in humanitarianism, in science if not in justice. And at the same time he knows that his whole life is based on conditions that are directly contrary to all the principles of Christianity, humanitarianism, justice and science.

He knows that the whole way of life in which he has been brought up, and which it would be a great hardship for him to abandon, can only be maintained by the painful, often injurious, labour of the oppressed workers, that is, by the most obvious and glaring contradiction of the very principles of Christianity, humanitarianism, justice or science (I refer to political economy) that he himself claims to follow. He professes the principles of brotherhood, humanitarianism, justice or science, yet lives in such a way as to be unable to do without the oppression of the workers he so disapproves of. His whole life constitutes an exploitation of this oppression, and all his activities are directed towards the maintenance of a social order directly contrary to all he believes in.

We are all brothers, yet every morning a brother or sister carries out my chamber-pot. We are all brothers, yet every morning I need a cigar, some sugar, a mirror and other objects produced by my equals, my own brothers and sisters, at the cost of their own health; I make use of these objects and even demand them. We are all brothers, yet I work in a bank, firm or shop, earning my living from increasing the price of articles needed by my own brothers. We are all brothers, yet I live on a salary that I receive for detecting, judging and punishing thieves or prostitutes, people whose existence is a consequence of my whole way of life, and who I know should be corrected rather than punished. We are all brothers, yet I live on a salary that I receive for collecting taxes from poor workers for the benefit of the idle rich. We are all brothers, yet I receive a salary for preaching a pseudo-Christian faith in which I do not believe myself, and which makes it impossible for people to recognize the true faith. I receive a salary as a clergyman or bishop for deceiving people in matters that are more important than anything else in life. We are all brothers, yet I only give my educational, medical and literary works to the poor in exchange for money. We are all brothers, yet I receive a salary for making preparations for murder, for learning to kill, for manufacturing weapons or explosives or building fortresses.

The whole life of our upper classes is one unrelieved contradiction, a contradiction that is all the more painful to those whose moral consciousness is more sensitive.

A man with a sensitive conscience cannot but suffer if he lives such a life. The only way for him to escape this suffering is to stifle his conscience, but even if he succeeds in doing this he will be unable to stifle his fear.

The less sensitive members of the oppressor classes, together with those who have managed to stifle their conscience, suffer instead from fear and hatred. It is impossible for them not to suffer. They are aware of the hatred that the workers feel, and cannot not feel towards them. They are aware that the workers know they have been deceived and raped, and that they are beginning to organize themselves in order to throw off the burden of oppression and take their revenge. The upper classes see workers' unions, strikes and May-Day celebrations, and sense the impending disaster; the fear they then experience poisons their lives, changing as it does into defensiveness and hatred. They know that if they weaken for one minute in their struggle against the oppressed slaves, then they themselves will perish – since the slaves are embittered, and more embittered with every day. Even if they should wish to, the oppressors cannot cease to oppress. They know they will perish the minute they even relax their oppression, let alone bring it to an end. And so they act accordingly – in spite of any apparent concern they may show for the welfare of the workers, for eight-hour days, for wages and pensions and the prohibition of labour by women and children. All this is either a deceit or else it springs from a concern that the slave should remain strong enough to do his work; the slave remains a slave and the master – unable to live without him – less than ever in a position to release him.

The governing classes are in the same position with regard to the workers as a man who has brought his adversary to the floor and cannot let him go, not because he does not wish to, but because he knows that his opponent is embittered and carrying a knife in his hand. He knows that if he releases him for even a moment, he will himself immediately be stabbed. And so, whether they are sensitive or insensitive, our wealthy classes are unable – like the ancients who believed in their rights – to enjoy the good things they have stolen from the poor. All their life and all their pleasures are poisoned either by fear or by the voice of conscience.

Something even more striking, however, than this economic contradiction, is the political contradiction. Everyone is brought up to obey the laws of the State. The entire life of people of our time is determined by these laws. A man marries and divorces, brings up children or even – in many countries – professes a particular faith, in accordance with the law. What is this law that determines people's lives? Do they believe in it? Do they consider it to be a true law? Not in the least!

In most cases people of our time do not believe in the justice of the law; they despise it and yet still obey it. It was all very well for the men of antiquity to obey their laws. They believed, truly believed, that their law, usually a religious law, was the one true law which everyone should obey. But what about us? We are aware, and cannot help be aware, that not only is the law of our State not the one and only eternal law, but that it is merely one of the many laws made by different governments, all equally imperfect, some of them obviously false and unjust, that are subject to discussion in the press.

It was all very well for a Jew to obey his laws when he had no doubt that they were written by the finger of God. It was all very well for a Roman who thought that his laws had been written by the nymph Egeria. It was all very well when people believed that the kings who made the laws were the anointed of God, even when they believed that their legislative assemblies truly wished, and had the ability, to draw up the best possible laws. But we all know only too well how laws are made, we have all been behind the scenes, we know that laws are the product of greed, deceit and party struggle, that there is no justice in them and never can be any. And so it is impossible for people of our time to believe that obedience to the civil and State laws is enough to satisfy the human demand for reason. People have known for a long time that it is irrational to obey a law whose justice is doubtful; they cannot but suffer when they obey a law which they do not recognize as reasonable and binding.

A man cannot but suffer when the course of his entire life is predetermined by laws which he must obey under threat of punishment, laws which he not only cannot recognize as fair and reasonable but which he often clearly recognizes to be harsh, unfair and unnatural. We recognize the uselessness of customs and import duties yet have to pay them. We recognize that the money spent on the upkeep of the Court and many grades of the administration is useless; we recognize that the teachings of the Church are harmful; and yet we have to contribute to the upkeep of both these organizations. We recognize that the punishments decreed by courts are harsh and merciless, yet we have to play our part in applying them. We recognize that the system of land distribution is wrong and harmful, yet have to accept it. We do not recognize the necessity of armies and laws, yet have to bear terrible burdens in order to help maintain armies and wage wars.

But even this contradiction is nothing compared with the contradiction that demands to be resolved in international relations, the contradiction between Christian consciousness and war that now threatens human reason and even human life.

We are all Christian nations living one spiritual life, so that every good and fruitful thought arising at one end of the world, immediately communicated to all Christendom, evokes the same feelings of joy and pride in us all irrespective of nationality. We love not only the thinkers, benefactors, poets and men of science of other nations, taking pride in the achievements of Father Damian as if they were our own, but we also have a straightforward love of all people of other nationalities whether French, German, American or English. We not only respect their good qualities but are glad when we meet them and greet them with a smile. Not only are we unable to look on war with these people as an achievement; but we are unable to think without horror of the possibility of a disagreement between them and us that could only be resolved by mutual killing. And yet we are all of us called to play our part in this killing, which will inevitably take place, tomorrow if not today.

It was fine for the Jew, the Greek and the Roman to use slaughter not only to uphold the independence of his own nation, but even to subordinate other nations. He, after all, believed that his was the only true, good and fine people beloved of God, and that all others were philistines and barbarians. Such beliefs were still possible in the Middle Ages, even at the end of the last century and the very beginning of the present century. But we, however much we are provoked, are unable to believe such things, and the contradiction has become so terrible that it is impossible for the people of our time to live without a resolution of it.

The First Step

No collection of Tolstoy's religious writings could omit his preoccupation with eating meat. As has been said, he was a vegetarian (with a few lapses) from 1880 until the day of his death in 1910. He does not claim that Jesus was a vegetarian. But by the time he wrote *The First Step*, in 1891, Tolstoy had absorbed into his creed truths from other religions. In particular, he had studied the Buddhist scriptures, with great attention and profit.

The First Step

Fasting is a necessary condition of a good life; but in fasting, as in all exercises of self-restraint, we must answer the question of how to begin. How should we fast? How often should we eat, what should we eat and not eat? And just as we cannot do any work seriously without knowing the right order in which to go about it, so we cannot fast without knowing where to begin, where to begin practising self-restraint with regard to food.

Fasting! And even an analysis of how to do it! To most people this thought appears wildly ridiculous.

I remember how an evangelist who was attacking monasticism once said to me with obvious pride in his own originality: 'My Christianity goes not with fasting and deprivation, but with beef steaks.' Christianity, virtue in general, mixed with beef steaks!

So many wild and immoral ideas have eaten into the fabric of our lives, especially with regard to our attitude to food – that first and lowest of the steps towards a good life, a step which has received almost no attention – that it is difficult for us to understand the full senselessness and effrontery of this association of Christianity – or moral virtue – with beef steaks.

If we are not appalled by this, it is because something all too common has happened to us, because we look and do not see, because we hear and do not listen. There is no noise, no stench to which a man cannot grow accustomed, no horror which he cannot look on so often as not to notice what would astound anyone seeing it for the first time. It is the same with morals. Christianity and moral virtue mixed with beef steaks!

The other day I visited the slaughter-house in our town of

Tula. It is built in the same new and improved system as in the large cities, intended to spare the animals unnecessary suffering. I went on a Friday, two days before Trinity Sunday. There was a large number of cattle.

Long ago, when I was reading the splendid book, *The Ethics of Diet*, I had wanted to visit a slaughter-house, so as to see with my own eyes the truth of the accounts given by vegetarians. But I had felt guilty – as people always feel guilty looking at suffering they are unable to prevent – and I had kept putting it off.

But not long ago I met a butcher who was on his way back to Tula after visiting his home. He was still inexperienced and his job was to stab the animals with a knife. I asked him if he didn't feel sorry for the animals he killed. He gave the usual answer: 'Why should I feel sorry? It's something that has to be done.' But when I said that it wasn't necessary to eat meat, then he agreed and admitted that he did indeed feel sorry. 'But what else can I do? I have to earn my living. In the beginning I was *afraid* to kill. My father never in all his life killed so much as a chicken.' Most Russian people are unable to kill. They feel pity, though what they say is that they are *afraid*. He had been afraid too, but had got over it.

I also not long ago had a conversation with another butcher, a retired soldier. He was equally astonished at my saying that it was a pity to kill animals. Like everyone else he said that it was something ordained, but finally agreed: 'Especially when the animal's quiet and tame. When it's innocent and it trusts you. It does make me very sorry indeed.'

Once, when I was walking back from Moscow, I was given a lift by some carters from Serpukhov who were on their way to the forest to buy logs. It was the Thursday before Easter. I was in the first cart together with the carter, a strong, coarse man with a ruddy complexion and who obviously drank a lot. As we entered one village, we saw a well-fed, pink sow being dragged out of the first yard to be slaughtered. Its desperate squealing was very like a human scream. Just as we drove past, they began to slaughter the sow. One of the men slashed at her throat with a knife. She let out a still louder, more piercing squeal, broke free and ran off, covered in blood. I am short-sighted myself and was unable to see everything in detail; all I was aware of was the pink, almost human body of the sow and her desperate squeals. The carter, however, took in every detail without once looking away. They caught the pig, knocked it to the ground and began to finish it off. When its squeals came to an end, the carter let out a deep sigh.

People's revulsion at killing is very strong indeed. By follow-ing the example of others, however, encouraged by greed, by the claim that it is permitted by God and above all by habit, people succeed in entirely extinguishing this natural feeling.

On Friday I went to Tula. Meeting an acquaintance of mine, someone kind and meek, I asked him to go with me.

'Yes, I've heard it's very well organized and I've wanted to go and have a look. But if they're doing any slaughtering, I won't go in.'

'Why on earth not? That's just what I want to go and see. If one eats meat, then one must kill.'

'No, no, I can't.'

Something particularly remarkable is that this man was a hunter, someone who killed birds and wild animals himself.

We walked up to the building. Near the entrance hung a heavy, disgusting, fetid smell like carpenters' glue or a mixture of paint and glue. The closer we came, the stronger the smell.

It was a very large, red brick building, with vaults and tall chimneys. We went in through the gates. On the right was a large enclosed yard, about three-quarters of an acre, where twice a week the cattle for sale were herded; on the edge of this yard stood the caretaker's hut. On the left were what are called 'the chambers', rooms with round gates, sloping asphalt floors and contraptions for hanging and moving carcasses. On the bench against the wall of the caretaker's hut sat six butchers in aprons covered with blood, their blood-spattered sleeves rolled up over muscular arms. They had finished half an hour before, so all we were able to see then were the empty chambers. Although the gates were open on both sides, they were still filled with the heavy smell of warm blood. The floor was brown and shiny, its cavities full of blood that was congealed and black.

One of the butchers explained the process of slaughtering and showed us where it was done. I slightly misunderstood and formed a false, but horrible impression of the process. I thought that, as often happens, reality would make less of an impression on me than my imagination. In this I was wrong.

Next time I arrived punctually. This was the Friday before Trinity Sunday, a hot July day. The work was in full swing. The whole dusty yard was filled with cattle, as were the enclosures around the chambers.

Out on the street, before the entrance, stood carts with oxen, calves and cows tied to the shafts and the edges. Other carts were drawing up, pulled by fine horses; they were full of live calves whose heads hung down and swayed from side to side. Still more carts were drawing away, full of the carcasses of bullocks, with their heads, their bright red lungs and brown livers and their legs dangling out. Beside the fence stood the horses belonging to the cattle-dealers. The dealers themselves walked round the yard in their long frock-coats, whips and knouts in their hands, either marking cattle belonging to the same owner with tar, or bargaining, or else herding oxen and bulls from the yard into the enclosures on the way to the chambers. All these people were obviously entirely absorbed by questions of money and accounts; the question of whether or not it was right to kill these animals was as far from their minds as questions about the chemical composition of the blood covering the floor of the chambers.

There were no butchers to be seen in the yard; all of them were working in the chambers. That day about a hundred oxen were killed. I went into a chamber and stopped by the door. I stopped both because the chamber was entirely filled with carcasses being moved around, and because there was blood flowing across the floor and dripping down from above. All the butchers were smeared with blood and, if I had gone right in, I should have been smeared with it myself. One carcass was being taken down from where it was hanging, a second was being moved towards the door, a third – that of a bullock – was lying on the floor, its white legs up in the air, while a butcher ripped off the taut hide with his bare hands.

While I stood there, a large, red, well-fed ox was led in through the opposite door, dragged by two men. It was barely inside when I saw one of the butchers raise a knife over its neck and plunge it in. The ox immediately collapsed onto its stomach as though all four legs had been knocked from under it, rolled onto one side and began twitching its legs and hindquarters. Another butcher immediately threw himself onto the ox from the opposite side, grabbed its horns and held its head to the ground while a third butcher cut its throat. A stream of dark red blood gushed out from beneath the head and a blood-smeared boy placed a tin basin on the ground in order to catch it. While all this was going on, the ox was constantly twitching its head, as though trying to get up, and waving all four legs in the air. The basin was rapidly filling up, but the ox was still alive, its stomach heaving and its legs beating the air so that the butchers had to keep their distance. When the basin was full, the boy carried it away on his head to the albumen factory; another boy put down a second basin, which also began to fill up. The ox's stomach was still heaving and its back legs still in convulsions. When the blood stopped flowing, a butcher lifted the ox's head and began stripping off the hide. The ox continued to twitch. The naked head, red with white veins, now remained in whatever position it was placed by the butchers, the hide hanging down from either side. The ox was still twitching. Another butcher then grabbed one of the legs, broke it and cut it off. The stomach and the other legs were still shuddering. Next the other legs were cut off and thrown onto a heap of legs from oxen belonging to the same owner. The ox was then dragged to the hoist and strung up; it was no longer moving.

I stood by the door and watched as the same things happened to a second, third and fourth ox. Their heads were cut off with bitten tongues and their hindquarters went into convulsions. The only difference was that the slaughterer's aim was not always precise enough for the ox immediately to fall to the ground. Sometimes he missed, and the ox would leap up, bellow and attempt to escape, covered with blood as it was. It was then dragged under a beam; after being struck a second time, it fell to the ground.

I then went round and stood in the doorway through which the oxen were led in. What I saw was the same, only I could see more clearly. The main thing I had been unable to see before was how the oxen were forced to enter the chamber. Each time an ox was seized in the enclosure and dragged forward by a rope attached to its horns, it would smell blood and dig its heels in, sometimes bellowing and trying to step back. Two men could never have managed to drag it in by force, so one butcher walked behind, twisting its tail so violently that the cartilage cracked and the ox walked forward.

The oxen belonging to one owner came to an end and another man's cattle were brought in. The first of these was a bull, a fine, well-bred black bull with white markings and white legs, young, muscular and energetic. When he was dragged forward, he lowered his head and resisted determinedly. The butcher walking behind seized hold of his tail – like an engine-driver reaching for the handle of the whistle – and twisted it till the cartilage cracked. The bull rushed forward, knocking over the men holding the rope, and then dug his heels in again, looking sideways out of his black eyes that had filled with blood. Once again the tail cracked and the bull rushed forward to reach his appointed place. The slaughterer came up, took his aim and struck, missing the correct spot. The bull leaped up, shook his head, bellowed, broke free and leaped back, covered in blood. The people in the doorway all sprang out of the way, but the experienced butchers, with the panache of men accustomed to danger, quickly grabbed the rope. After another twist of his tail, the bull was back in the chamber and was finally dragged under the beam. In spite of all the blood the slaughterer quickly found the spot where the hair divides like a star and then struck; the splendid beast that had been so full of life fell to the ground, its head and legs continuing to shudder while it was bled and skinned.

'The accursed devil – it hasn't even fallen right!' grumbled the butcher who was cutting the skin from the head.

Five minutes later a naked head was sticking up, red instead of black, the eyes that had shone so brightly now glazed and fixed.

I then went into the section where the smaller animals were slaughtered. It was a very large, long room with an asphalt floor, and tables with backs on which the calves and sheep were killed. Here they had already finished work; the room was impregnated with the smell of blood, and there were only two butchers still there. One was blowing into the leg of a dead lamb and slapping its inflated stomach with the palm of one hand; the other, a young fellow in a frock-coat spattered with blood, was smoking a bent cigarette. They were the only people in this long, gloomy room that was filled with such a heavy smell. After me someone who looked like a retired soldier came in, carrying a black yearling lamb with a white mark on its neck and its legs tied. He placed the lamb on one of the tables as though on a bed. The soldier, evidently an acquaintance, greeted the butchers and began asking when their boss let them go. The young fellow with the cigarette walked up with a knife which he sharpened on the edge of the table, and said that they were free on feast days. The lamb was lying just as quietly as the dead, blown-up lamb, except that it was very quickly wagging its short tail and that its sides were heaving more rapidly than usual. The soldier very gently pressed down the head it was beginning to raise up; the young fellow, continuing to talk, took hold of the lamb's head with his left hand and cut its throat. The lamb quivered and the tail stiffened and stopped wagging. The young man relit his cigarette as he waited for the blood to drain. The blood flowed and the lamb went into convulsions. The conversation went on without the least interruption.

And what about the hens and chickens which every day, in thousands of kitchens, jump about with their heads cut off, covered in blood and flapping their wings, at once both comic and terrible?

And then a kind, refined young lady will devour the corpses of these animals, certain that she is doing the right thing as she makes two mutually contradictory assertions:

Firstly that she is so delicate – as her doctor assures her – that she cannot survive on vegetable food since her weak organism needs meat; secondly that she is so sensitive as to be unable not only to cause suffering to animals, but even to bear the sight of it.

But the only reason for the poor young lady being weak is that she has been taught to eat food that is unnatural for man; and it is impossible for her not to cause suffering to animals because she devours them.

CHAPTER TEN

We cannot pretend that we do not know this. We are not ostriches, and we cannot believe that if we close our eyes, then what we do not want to see will not happen. This is all the more impossible when what we wish to close our eyes to is what we eat.

If all this were necessary, it would be different. Or even if it were in any way useful. But it is not. Its only effect is to encourage animal feelings and to increase lust, fornication and drunkenness. This is repeatedly confirmed by the fact that young, kind, unspoiled people, especially women and girls, can sense, without knowing why, that virtue and beef steaks are incompatible. When they wish to be virtuous, they give up meat.

What then do I wish to say? That people who wish to be moral should give up meat? Not in the least!

I only wish to say that a certain sequence of right actions is a prerequisite to a good life; that if a man is serious in his aspiration towards a good life, then his actions must follow a particular sequence; and that in this sequence the first virtue that a man must strive to cultivate is self-control, self-mastery.

In developing self-control a man must also follow a particular sequence of actions – and the first object with regard to which he will learn to practise self-control is food. If he is seriously and sincerely seeking a good life, the first thing he will abstain from in his fasting is animal food. Leaving aside the fact that animal food excites the passions, its consumption is quite simply immoral since it requires something contrary to all sense of morality – the act of killing – and is necessitated only by our greed and our desire for delicacies.

Why abstinence from animal food must be the first act of fasting and of a moral life has been excellently explained not by one person alone but by all the finest representatives of humanity throughout its conscious life.

'But why, if the unlawfulness of eating animal food has been known to humanity for so long, have people still not come to recognize this law?' is a question that will be asked by people who are usually guided not so much by their own reason as by public opinion. The answer is that humanity's moral progress – the foundation of all other progress – has always been extremely slow, but that a characteristic of true progress is that it cannot be stopped and that it constantly accelerates.

The progress of vegetarianism does indeed show these characteristics. This progress is shown both in the thoughts of people who have written on this subject and in the life of humanity as a whole, which, at an unconscious level, is tending more and more towards a vegetable diet at the same time as it is deliberately moving that way in the form of the strong and continually expanding vegetarian movement. During the last ten years this movement has grown increasingly rapidly. Every year more and more books and journals are published; every year one meets more and more people who abstain from meat; and in other countries, especially in Germany, England and America, the number of vegetarian hotels and restaurants increases every year.

This movement should bring especial joy to those who aspire to realize the Kingdom of God on earth, not because vegetarianism itself is such an important step towards this Kingdom (a true step is always both important and unimportant), but because it is an indication that man's aspiration towards moral perfection is both serious and sincere, since it is now following the natural and unalterable sequence of steps, beginning with the first.

One cannot fail to rejoice at this – any more than people wishing to reach the top of a house could fail to rejoice if, after trying haphazardly and unsuccessfully to climb straight up the walls, they finally met together by the first step of the staircase, crowding towards it, aware that there is no other way up.

The Destruction of
Hell and Its Restoration

Tolstoy wrote this instructive little tale in 1903. It is a mistake to regard Tolstoy as a purely solemn man. In photographs he always tends to look stern and tormented, and the bulk of his writing is deeply serious. But it is frequently enlivened by humour, and we are told that when he was on good form there were a lot of laughs to be had in his company. This spirited and humorous tale contains the whole essence of Tolstoy's religion, and offers a view of Church Christianity which it is difficult to dispute.

The Destruction of
Hell and Its Restoration

A LEGEND

This happened when Christ was revealing His teaching to men.
This teaching was so clear, so easy to follow; it so obviously
delivered men from evil that it was impossible not to accept it.
Nothing could stop it from spreading throughout the entire
world. Beelzebub, the father and ruler of all the devils, was
troubled. He could clearly see that unless Christ renounced His
teaching, his own power over men would be for ever ended. He
was troubled, but instead of falling into despair he encouraged
his servants the scribes and Pharisees to insult and torment
Christ for all they were worth. At the same time he advised the
disciples of Christ to escape and abandon Him. He hoped that,
after being sentenced to a shameful death, after being reviled,
after being abandoned by all His disciples, and after undergo-
ing the agony of the crucifixion itself, Christ would at the last
moment renounce His teaching. He hoped that this renuncia-
tion would destroy all its power.

It was on the Cross that all this was decided. When Christ
exclaimed, 'My God, my God, why hast thou forsaken me?',
Beelzebub exulted. He seized the fetters that had been got
ready, put them on his own legs and adjusted them so that once
they had been put on the legs of Christ they could never again
be undone.

But then came the words, 'Father, forgive them, for they
know not what they do.' And after that Christ cried, 'It is
finished', and gave up the ghost.

Beelzebub realized that all was lost. He wanted to remove

the fetters from his legs, but was unable to move. The fetters were welded onto him, binding his legs. He wanted to use his wings to fly, but was unable to open them. Then Beelzebub saw Christ at the gates of Hell, surrounded by a halo of light. He saw how all the sinners, from Adam to Judas, came out, how the devils ran off in all directions, how the walls of Hell silently collapsed on all four sides. Unable to bear all this, he let out a piercing shriek and disappeared through the gaping floor of Hell into the lower regions.

II

A hundred years passed by, two hundred, three hundred.

Beelzebub did not count the time. He lay without moving, surrounded by black gloom and deathly silence, trying not to think about what had happened. Unable not to think about it, he was filled with impotent hatred for the man who had brought about his ruin.

But suddenly – he had no idea how many hundred years had passed – he heard above him something that sounded like the tramping of feet, groans, cries and the gnashing of teeth.

Beelzebub lifted up his head a little and began to listen.

That Hell could have been restored after the victory of Christ was more than he could believe. But he could hear the tramping, the groans, the cries and the gnashing of teeth more and more clearly.

Beelzebub raised himself up, doubled up his shaggy legs with their unkempt hooves (his fetters, to his amazement, had dropped off all by themselves), opened out his wings, flapped them, and gave the whistle by which in former times he had called his servants and helpers.

He had barely drawn his breath when an opening appeared above his head. There was a flash of red flame, and a crowd of devils, crushing against one another, dropped out of the opening into the lower regions. They settled in a circle around Beelzebub like crows around carrion.

There were big devils and little devils, fat devils and thin devils, devils with long tails and devils with short tails, devils with pointed horns, devils with bent horns and devils with straight horns.

One of them, a shiny black devil who was quite naked except for a cape thrown over his shoulders, with a round, hairless face and a vast, drooping paunch, was squatting right in front of Beelzebub. He was rolling his flaming eyes up and down, waving his long, thin tail rhythmically from side to side, and smiling, continually smiling.

III

'What does that noise mean?' said Beelzebub, pointing up above. 'What's going on?'

'The same as always has gone on', answered the shiny devil in the cape.

'So there really are sinners?' asked Beelzebub.

'Lots of them', answered the shiny devil.

'And what about the teaching of a man I prefer not to name?' asked Beelzebub.

The devil in the cape bared his sharp teeth in a grin while the other devils let out suppressed laughs.

'The teaching doesn't bother us. They don't believe in it', said the devil in the cape.

'But the teaching all too clearly delivers them from us. He bore witness to it with His own death', said Beelzebub.

'I altered it', said the devil in the cape, tapping his tail rapidly against the floor.

'How?'

'So that people believe not in His teaching, but in my own, which they call by His name.'

'How did you do that?' asked Beelzebub.

'It happened by itself. I just helped.'

'Tell me a little', said Beelzebub.

The devil in the cape lowered his head and fell silent for a while as though lost in thought. Then he began.

'After those terrible events, after Hell had been destroyed and our father and ruler had left us, I went to visit the places where the teaching which so nearly ruined us had been spread. I wanted to see the life of the people who followed it. I soon realized that they were entirely happy and quite beyond our grasp. They didn't get angry with one another, they didn't succumb to the charms of women, and they either kept to one wife or didn't marry at all. They held everything in common and owned no property, they didn't use force to defend themselves, and they repaid evil with good. Their life was so fine that other people were more and more attracted to them. I thought that everything was lost and I almost left. But then something happened, something quite insignificant in itself but which seemed worth my attention. And so I remained.

'Some of these people believed that everyone should be circumcized, and that one should not eat food that had been offered to idols. Others believed that circumcision was quite unnecessary, and that it was all right to eat anything. I began to suggest to both sides that this disagreement was of extreme importance, and that since it concerned the service of God, it was imperative that they did not give in. They believed me, and their arguments grew more bitter. Each side grew angry with the other, and I suggested to them that they could prove the truth of their teaching by miracles. Obvious though it is that miracles cannot prove the truth of a teaching, they so much wanted to be in the right that they believed me, and I arranged them some miracles. It wasn't difficult. They were ready to believe anything that would confirm them as the sole possessors of truth.

'Some said that tongues of fire had come down on them, others that they had seen the dead teacher Himself, and many other things. They made up all kinds of things that had never happened; without realizing it, in the name of Him who called us liars, they lied no worse than we do ourselves. One side said to the other: "Your miracles aren't true miracles, but ours are." The other side said: "No, it is ours that are the only true miracles."

'Things were going well, but I was afraid that they might see through this rather obvious deception, and so I thought up the

Church. When they believed in that, I felt calm. I knew that we were saved and that Hell was restored.'

IV

'What is "the Church"?' asked Beelzebub severely, reluctant to believe that his servants could be more clever than he was himself.

'Well, when people lie and know that no one believes them, they always call on God, saying, "By God, what I say is the truth!" Really, the Church is just like that, except that the people who call themselves the Church really do believe they can never be wrong. And so, whatever nonsense they come out with, they can never take it back. The Church is formed in the following way: people convince themselves and others that their teacher, God, wishing to avoid any misinterpretation of the law He has revealed, has chosen certain people who alone, together with those to whom they pass on this power, have the ability to interpret His teaching. And so the people who call themselves the Church look on themselves as possessors of truth, not because what they preach is true, but because they think they are the only legitimate heirs of the disciples of the disciples of the disciples of the disciples of the teacher who was God. Although this method does have the same disadvantage as the miracles, that a number of people can each claim at the same time to be members of the one true Church – as indeed has always been the case – it also has the advantage that as soon as people found their teaching on the claim that they themselves embody the Church, then they are unable to take back anything they say, however absurd it may be and whatever other people may say.'

'But what made the Church misinterpret the teachings in our favour?' asked Beelzebub.

'Once they had proclaimed themselves as the only interpreters of the law of God, and once they had convinced others of this, these people became the supreme judges of people's fates and so obtained supreme power over them. Once they possessed this power, they naturally grew arrogant, and in most cases depraved, and so aroused people's indignation and enmity. Having no other weapons against their enemies except violence, they took to persecuting, executing and burning anyone who did not accept their power. The very position they had taken up forced them to misinterpret the teaching so as to justify their evil ways and the cruel methods they employed against their enemies. And that is just what they did.'

V

'But the teaching was so simple and so clear,' said Beelzebub, still not wishing to believe that his servants could have done something he had never even thought of himself, 'as to be incapable of misinterpretation: "Do unto others as you would that they should do unto you" – how can that be misinterpreted?'

'On my advice,' replied the devil in the cape, 'a number of different methods were used. Men have a story about a good magician who turned a man into a grain of millet in order to save him from an evil magician. The evil magician turned himself into a cock and was about to peck up the grain when the good magician emptied out a whole sack of other grains. The evil magician was unable to eat up all the grain, nor could he find the one grain he wanted. The same thing was done, on my advice, with the teaching that the whole of the law lies in doing unto others as you wish them to do unto you; forty-nine books were accepted as the sacred exposition of the law of God, and every word of these books was seen as the word of God the Holy Ghost. Over the one simple and incomprehensible truth they poured such a heap of false truths that it became equally impossible to accept them all or to find the one truth that we need. This was their first method.

'The second method, used with success for over a thousand years, was simply to murder and burn anyone who wished to reveal the truth. Although this method is now going out of use, it has not yet been entirely abandoned; although they no longer burn people, they poison their lives, slandering them so fiercely that only a very few people dare to stand up to them.

'The third method is as follows. Since they are the Church and therefore infallible, they are able to proclaim the opposite of what has been written in the Scriptures, leaving their pupils to find their own way out of these contradictions. In the Scriptures, for example, it is written: "Call no man your father upon the earth: for one is your Father, which is in Heaven. Neither be ye called masters: for one is your master, even Christ" (Matthew 23:9–10; A.V.). In spite of this, these people say: "We alone are fathers and we alone are masters of men." Again, it is written: "When thou prayest, do so in secret, and God will hear thee" (Matthew 6:6). They, however, teach men to pray in churches, all together, with singing and music. It is written: "Swear not at all." They, however, teach that people must swear unconditional obedience to the authorities, whatever the demands they impose. It is written: "Thou shalt not kill" (Exodus 21:13). They, however, teach that one can and must kill during wars and executions. It is written: "My teaching is spirit and life. Feed upon it as upon bread." They, however, teach that if you dip pieces of bread in wine and say certain words over them, then the bread will become flesh and the wine become blood; and if you eat this bread and drink this wine, it will help to save your soul. People believe all this and diligently eat their sops; they are astonished when they end up with us to find that these sops have been of no help whatsoever.'

The devil in the cape came to an end, rolling his eyes and grinning from ear to ear.

'All this is excellent', said Beelzebub with a smile. The devils all burst into loud laughter.

VI

'So do you really have fornicators, robbers and murderers, just like before?' asked Beelzebub, now speaking quite gaily.

The devils, also growing more animated, began talking all at once, each of them trying to show off before Beelzebub.

'No, not like before!' shouted one devil. 'There are more of them than before!'

'There isn't enough room in the old part for all the adulterers', squealed another.

'And robbers now are much worse than they used to be', shouted a third.

'We can't get enough fuel for all the murderers', bellowed a fourth.

'Don't all talk at once. I want the person I question to reply, and no one else. Whoever is in charge of vice, come forward and tell me what you do with the pupils of the teacher who forbade men to change their wives or even to look on another woman with lust. Who is in charge of vice?'

'I am', replied an effeminate brown devil, as he shuffled towards Beelzebub on his bottom. He had a flabby face and slobbering jaws that were constantly in motion. He squatted in front of the other devils, bent his head to one side, tucked his tufted tail between his legs, waved it about, and began in a sing-song voice:

'We use both the old way, the way that you, our father and ruler, employed in Paradise in order to deliver the whole human race into our hands, and a new ecclesiastical way. Let me tell you about the new ecclesiastical way: we convince people that marriage is not a matter of the coupling of man and woman, but a matter of dressing up in one's finest clothes, going into a large building that has been decorated for the occasion, putting special hats on one's head and circling three times around a small table to the accompaniment of various songs. We make people believe that this alone constitutes a true marriage. As a result, they naturally think that any other coupling of man and woman is just the satisfaction of a physical need, a simple pleasure that brings with it no obligations. And they give themselves up to this simple pleasure without restraint.'

The effeminate devil bent his head to the other side and fell silent, as though waiting for Beelzebub's reaction.

Beelzebub nodded his head in approval and the devil continued: 'It is by this method, not forgetting the earlier method employed in Paradise, that of curiosity and the forbidden fruit,' he continued, obviously hoping to flatter Beelzebub, 'that we gain our finest successes. Under the illusion that they can arrange an honest church marriage for themselves even after they have known a large number of women, people change their wives hundreds of times. They grow so used to this that they go on doing the same even after they have got married. If they feel constrained by some of the demands that go with a church marriage, then they arrange to have another walk round the little table, the first one being proclaimed invalid.'

The effeminate devil fell silent. Wiping his slobbering mouth with the end of his tail, he bent his head to the other side and stared at Beelzebub.

VII

'Very simple and very good', said Beelzebub. 'You have my approval. And who is in charge of the robbers?'

'I am.' A large devil came forward, with big, crooked horns, a moustache that pointed upwards, and huge, equally crooked paws. He crawled to the front like the other one and arranged his moustache military fashion with both paws, waiting to be questioned.

'The man who destroyed Hell', said Beelzebub, 'taught men to live like the birds of heaven, saying that one must give one's coat to a man who demands one's shirt, and that one must give away all one's possessions in order to be saved. How do you inveigle men who have heard that into robbery?'

'We do it', said the devil with the moustache, throwing his head back loftily, 'in the same way our father and ruler did when Saul was chosen to be king. We make people think, just as you did then, that instead of all ceasing to rob one another it would be easier if they all allow themselves to be robbed by a single man to whom they grant absolute power. The only novelty in our method is our way of confirming this man's right to steal. We lead him into a church, place a special hat on his head, sit him on a tall chair, place a stick and a ball in his hands, smear him with vegetable oil and proclaim, in the name of God the Father and God the Son, that now he has been smeared with oil his person is sacred. After this, since he is considered sacred, there can be no restrictions on the amount that he steals. And so these sacred persons, together with their assistants and their assistants' assistants, continue quietly to plunder the people, not incurring the least danger. At the same time they lay down laws and regulations which allow an idle minority to steal from the labouring majority without fear of punishment. Some States have recently come to allow this robbery to continue in exactly the same way without anyone being anointed. As our father and ruler can see, the method we employ is in essence the same old method as always. All that is new is that we have made this method more general, more hidden, more extended in space and time, and also more stable.

'The way we have made it more general is as follows. Previously people submitted of their own free will to someone they had chosen themselves. We, however, have arranged things so that they submit, regardless of their own will, to anyone at all.

'We have made it more hidden in that the people who are robbed, thanks to the system of indirect taxation, no longer see anything of their robbers.

'The method is more extended in space in that the so-called Christians, not satisfied with robbing their own people, also rob all foreign peoples who possess anything worth stealing. This they carry out under the strangest of pretexts, chiefly that of propagating Christianity. And the method is more extended in time thanks to the system of public and State loans. It is now not only the living who are robbed, but also generations to come.

'And the method is more stable in so far as the chief robbers are considered sacred persons, and therefore no one dares to oppose them. The chief robber only has to have himself smeared with oil, and he can calmly steal to his heart's content from whomever he wants. Once, as an experiment, I placed on the Russian throne some of the most vile women, one after another, women who were stupid, illiterate and depraved and who, according to their own laws, had no right to be there. The last of them was not only depraved but also a criminal, someone who had killed her own husband and legitimate heir. And because she had been smeared with oil, people not only failed to tear out her nostrils and flog her – which is what they usually did to women who had murdered their husbands – but instead were slavishly obedient to her for thirty years, allowing her and her countless lovers to steal not only their property but also their freedom.

'And so nowadays open robbery – taking someone's purse, horse or clothes – constitutes barely a millionth part of the legitimate robberies that are carried out every day by everyone who has the power. Nowadays hidden, unpunishable robbery, the willingness to rob, have become so well established as to become the main aim in life of nearly everyone, moderated only by conflicts between the robbers themselves.'

VIII

'Well, that is good', said Beelzebub. 'But what about murder? Who is in charge of murder?'

'I am', answered a blood-red devil as he stepped out from the crowd. He had fangs that stuck out from his mouth, pointed horns and a thick tail that pointed upwards without moving.

'How do you make murderers out of the disciples of the man who said: "Do not render evil for evil, but love your enemies"? What do you do to make them into murderers?'

'We use the old method', answered the red devil in a deafening voice, 'of exciting avarice, discord, hatred, vengeance and pride. And we still persuade the teachers of men that the best way for them to deter men from murder is publicly to murder all murderers. This doctrine, however, serves not so much to turn men into murderers as to prepare them for it.

'What gave us the largest number of murderers in the past is the doctrine of the infallibility of the Church. Those who saw themselves as members of an infallible Church considered it criminal to allow false interpreters of the teaching to pervert others; they saw the murder of such people as a service to God. And so they murdered whole populations, burning and executing hundreds of thousands of people. The amusing part is that it is our most dangerous enemies, those who were beginning to understand the true teaching, who were considered to be servants of the Devil and so were condemned to be executed and burnt at the stake. Whereas those who condemned them, who really were our obedient servants, saw themselves as the holy executors of the will of God.

'That's how things used to be, but what gives us a very large number of murderers nowadays is the teaching of Christian marriage and also that of equality. The teaching of marriage brings about both the murder of one spouse by another, and the murder of children by their mothers. Husbands and wives kill one another when the customs of church marriage and certain demands of the law begin to seem a restriction. Mothers kill their children for the main part when they are the fruit of unions not recognized by marriage. These kinds of murder occur very regularly.

'Murders brought about by the teaching of equality, on the other hand, occur only irregularly, but when they do occur they occur in large numbers. According to this teaching, all people are equal before the law. People who have been robbed feel that this is not the case. They can see that this equality only makes it easy for the robbers to continue to rob, while making it difficult for them to do the same; as a result they indignantly attack their plunderers. And then mutual murder begins, something which can give us tens of thousands of murders all at once.'

IX

'But what about the murder of war? How do you entice people to war when they have learnt the teaching of Him who taught men to love their enemies, saying that they were all sons of one father?'

The red devil grinned, letting out a stream of fire and smoke from his mouth, and joyfully slapped himself on the back with his thick tail.

'This is what we do. We persuade each people that it is the very best in the entire world – *Deutschland über Alles*, France, England, *Russia über Alles* – and that it is the duty of this people – their name is legion – to hold power over all others. Since they have all been imbued with the same ideas, they all think they are in danger from their neighbours, and make constant, embittered preparations for self-defence. And the more one country prepares to defend itself against the neighbours it hates, the more these neighbours do likewise. And so now all the people who accepted the teaching of Him who called us murderers are continually and for most of their time engaged either in preparations for murder or in murder itself.'

X

'Well, that is intelligent', said Beelzebub after a short silence. 'But how is it that scholars untouched by all this deception have failed to see that the Church has corrupted the teaching? Why is it they have not re-established it?'

'Because they are unable to', said a matt-black devil in a self-assured voice. He crawled forward, dressed in a mantle. He had a flat, sloping forehead, large, protruding ears and etiolated limbs.

'Why is that?' asked Beelzebub severely, irritated by the devil's self-assured tone of voice.

Not in the least embarrassed by Beelzebub's question, the devil in the mantle calmly sat down in the oriental fashion, crossing his puny legs instead of squatting as the others had done. Without the least hesitation he began to speak in a quiet, measured tone of voice.

'They are unable to do that because I distract their attention from what they can know and need to know, and divert it to what they do not need to know and can never know.'

'And how do you do that?'

'I use different methods at different times. In the past I used to persuade people that what mattered more than anything else was to know details about the relationship between the three persons of the Trinity, about the origin of Christ and His natures, about the attributes of God and so on. All this they discussed at great length, arguing, quarrelling and growing angry with one another. They became so absorbed by these discussions that they gave no thought whatsoever to their manner of life. As a result they no longer needed even to know what their teacher had said about life.

'Later on, when they had grown so confused in their arguments that they no longer had any idea what they were talking about, I persuaded some people that what mattered most of all was to study and explicate everything that had been written thousands of years ago by a Greek called Aristotle. I persuaded others that what mattered most of all was to find a stone which they could use to make gold, and also an elixir which would heal all illnesses and make people immortal. And so the most intelligent and learned men devoted all their intellectual powers to these questions.

'I persuaded other people, who were not interested in these questions, that what mattered was to find out whether the earth span round the sun, or the sun round the earth. When they learned that it was the earth which moved and not the sun, and had worked out how many millions of miles it was from the earth to the sun, they felt very pleased with themselves indeed. Since then they have been studying the distances between the stars with even greater diligence, although they are aware that there is no end to these distances, and that the number of stars is infinite, and that there is no need whatsoever for them to know all this. I also made people think that it was very important to find out the origin of all the animals, all the worms, all the plants and all the tiniest creatures. And although it is clearly equally unnecessary and impossible to find out such things – since the number of animals and other creatures is as infinite as that of the stars – they still devote all their intellectual powers to such investigations of material phenomena, con- stantly expressing astonishment that the more unnecessary things they learn, the more remain to be learned. Although it is obvious that the more studies they carry out, the more the realm of what remains to be studied tends to expand, and the more complicated grow the objects of study, and the more irrelevant and inapplicable their knowledge becomes to life – although this is obvious, it does not worry them in the least. Convinced of the importance of their activities, they continue to research, to teach, to write, to publish and translate debates and investigations that for the most part are of no practical value. And if on occasion their activities do have a practical application, it is always one that tends to increase the comfort of the rich minority or to aggravate the condition of the poor.

'To prevent these men from ever guessing that the one thing they need is the establishment of the laws of life indicated in the teachings of Christ, I persuade them that the laws of the life of the soul are unknowable, that any religious teaching – including that of Christ – is an error and superstition, and that they can best learn how they should live from sociology, a science I have thought up myself and whose object is to study the various bad ways of life led in the past. As a result, instead of following Christ's teaching and attempting to live better, they think that all they need to do is to study the lives of people now dead, and deduce various general laws of life; all that remains is then to bring their lives into conformity with these laws.

'In order to confirm them still deeper in error, I persuade them of something similar to the teaching of the Church, that there is a particular tradition of knowledge called science and that its claims, like those of the Church, are infallible.

'And so, as soon as the leading figures in science are convinced of their infallibility, they naturally proclaim as indubitable truths things that are not only unnecessary but often even absurd. And once they have said them, they are unable to take them back.

'It is for these reasons that I say that as long as I continue to inspire people with a respectful servility towards the science I have devised for them, they will never be able to understand the teaching that almost led to our ruin.'

XI

'Very good. Thank you', said Beelzebub, his face shining. 'You deserve a reward and I shall give you what is due.'

'But you've forgotten about us!' shouted all the other devils in their different voices, big devils and small devils, bandy-legged devils, fat devils and thin devils, all of them with fur of different colour.

'What do you do?' asked Beelzebub.

'I'm the devil of technical improvements.'

'I'm the devil of the division of labour.'

'I'm the devil of means of communication.'

'I'm the devil of printing.'

'I'm the devil of art.'

'I'm the devil of medicine.'

'I'm the devil of culture.'

'I'm the devil of education.'

'I'm the devil of reforming people.'

'I'm the devil of intoxication.'

'I'm the devil of philanthropy.'

'I'm the devil of socialism.'

'I'm the devil of feminism.'

They all shouted at once, pressing forward in front of Beelzebub.

'Speak briefly and one at a time', shouted Beelzebub. 'You!' he said, turning to the devil of technical improvements. 'What do you do?'

'I persuade people that the more things they make, and the more quickly, the better it will be for everyone. And so people ruin their lives in order to produce things, making more and more of them in spite of the fact that they are neither needed by those who have them made, nor available to those who make them.'

'Good. And what about you?' Beelzebub turned to the devil of the division of labour.

'I persuade people that since things can be made more quickly by machines than by people, then people must be transformed into machines. The people who are transformed into machines then hate the people who have done this to them.'

'That's very good too. And what about you?' Beelzebub turned to the devil of means of communication.

'I persuade people that they need to move about as quickly as possible from place to place. Instead of bettering their life at home, people spend most of their time travelling from place to place, taking great pride in the fact that they can travel thirty-five miles an hour and faster.'

Beelzebub praised him too.

The devil of printing came forward. He explained that his work lay in communicating to as many people as possible all the vile and stupid things that are done and written about in the world.

The devil of art explained that, while pretending to comfort people and inspire elevated feelings in them, he in fact pandered to their vices, depicting them in the most attractive manner.

The devil of medicine explained that his job was to convince people that the most important thing of all is to take care of one's own body. Since there is no end to caring for one's own body, people who concern themselves with it forget not only about the lives of others but even about their own.

The devil of culture explained that he persuaded people that it is almost a virtue to make use of everything provided by the devils of technical improvements, of the division of labour, of means of communication, of printing, of art, and of medicine; and that someone who uses all these things has a right to feel pleased with himself and not try to be any better.

The devil of education explained that he persuaded people that it is possible to teach children how to live well, while oneself living badly and not even knowing what constitutes a good life.

The devil of reforming explained that he taught people that they can reform the depraved even though they may be depraved themselves.

The devil of intoxication said that he taught people that instead of trying to live better, instead of trying to deliver themselves from the sufferings brought about by a bad way of life, it was better to seek self-oblivion under the influence of alcohol, tobacco, opium and morphine.

The devil of philanthropy said that he made people inaccessible to goodness by persuading them that if they gave back an ounce after stealing a hundredweight, then they were already virtuous and did not need to improve themselves.

The devil of socialism boasted that in the name of the highest degree of social organization he excited hostility between the classes.

The devil of feminism boasted that he excited hostility between the sexes in the name of a more perfect organization of social life.

'I am comfort! I am fashion!' still more devils cried and squealed as they crawled up to Beelzebub.

'Do you really think that I am so old and stupid as not to understand that if the teaching of life itself is false, then everything that would otherwise damage our interests instead goes to further them?' shouted Beelzebub with a loud peal of laughter. 'Enough of this! My thanks to you all!'

Beelzebub opened his wings and sprang to his feet. The devils surrounded him and began to form into a chain. At one end was the devil in a cape who had invented the Church; at the other end was the devil in a mantle who had invented science. These two held out their paws to one another and the circle was complete.

Then, chuckling, squealing, whistling and snorting, flicking and waving their tails, the devils began to whirl and spin around Beelzebub. Beelzebub himself danced in the middle, kicking his legs high into the air and flapping his spread wings. From above could be heard cries, wails, groans and the gnashing of teeth.

A Reply to
the Synod's Edict

After years in which he wrote only novellas, short stories and non-fiction, Tolstoy was stung into writing a full-length novel less by literary ambition than by simple pity. An eccentric religious sect, some of whose ideals were similar to his own, were suffering terrible persecution at the hands of the Imperial government. Four thousand Doukhobors, as these strange fanatics were called, were driven out of their villages by government troops, and their leaders were put in prison. Tolstoy was among the leaders of those who wanted to give these poor people their liberty. He therefore wrote *Resurrection*, a novel which he completed when he was seventy-one years old, and gave all the proceeds to help the Doukhobors emigrate to Canada. When the first shipload of Doukhobors (2134 of them) arrived in Canada on 21 December 1898, a Canadian called Bulmer made this speech to them: 'I do not know the name of your emperor, but the name of your patron and friend, Count Tolstoy, is as well known in Canada as in Russia, and I hope that one of the boys now listening to me, fifty years hence, will fill, like him, with honour to his country, the literary throne of their world.'

Resurrection is the story of how a rich man 'wrongs' a poor girl; of how she falls lower and lower in society until she becomes a prostitute, falsely accused of murder. Her seducer is a member of the jury, and the sight of her after many years creates in him a moral awakening which takes him in her footsteps to Siberia. The book contains Tolstoy's bitterest attacks on the government of the day, and his most satirical depictions of Orthodox piety. For this reason, the novel was instantly censored, but not before it had sold huge quantities in its doctored versions at home, and even larger quantities in translation abroad. By a strange irony, it was only in 1936 that a complete and unexpurgated version of the novel appeared in Russia, as part of the Jubilee Edition of Tolstoy's works. By then, conditions in Russia were even uglier than in the times of the Emperors. Religious eccentrics like the Doukhobors would have enjoyed little kindness from Stalin.

Church leaders, who had been wishing to get their own back for years, seized on Tolstoy's blasphemous descriptions of the Orthodox liturgy in *Resurrection*, and decreed that he should suffer the penalty of excommunication.

If this measure was intended to discredit Tolstoy with the Russian people, it had a very mixed success. At the time, a portrait of Tolstoy by Repin was on exhibit in a St Petersburg gallery. It depicted Tolstoy at prayer. 'Repin painted me barefooted in a shirt. I have to thank him for not having taken off my trousers as well', Tolstoy commented.

At the time of Tolstoy's excommunication, the authorities forbade any public demonstrations. But on the day it happened, crowds swarmed round this portrait and adorned it with flowers. It had become an icon.

What follows is Tolstoy's reply to the Holy Synod. It is a fair summary, written in his seventy-third year, of the creed by which he lived and in which he died, ten years later, in 1910.

A Reply to the Synod's Edict

What I believe is this: I believe in God, whom I understand as spirit, and in Love as the beginning of everything. I believe that the will of God is most clearly and understandably expressed in the teachings of the man called Christ, but I consider it the greatest of blasphemies to look on this man as God and to pray to Him. I believe that man's true good lies in following the will of God, and that God's will is for men to love one another and so do unto others as they wish others to do unto them; according to the gospels, this is the whole of the law and the prophets. I believe that the meaning of every man's life lies only in increasing the store of love within him; that this increase of love leads a man to greater and greater blessings in this life, and to blessings after his death that are in proportion to the amount of love within him; and I believe that it contributes more than anything else towards the establishment of the Kingdom of God on earth, that is, towards the establishment of an order under which the discord, deception and violence that now hold sway will be replaced by free agreement, truthfulness and brotherly love between all people. I believe that there is only one way to progress in love and that that is prayer: not the public prayer in churches that Christ expressly forbade (Matthew 6:5–13), but the solitary prayer of which Christ gave us an example and whose essence lies in the renewal and affirmation in our own consciousness of the meaning of our life and of our dependence on God alone.

Whether or not these beliefs of mine offend, grieve or tempt anyone, whether or not anyone dislikes them or finds them a hindrance, I am no more able to change them than I am able to change my own body. I have to live my own life and meet my own death – which I must do very soon – and so I cannot believe otherwise than I do now as I prepare to meet the God from whom I came. I do not say that mine is the one indubitable truth for all time, but I know of no other simpler, clearer truth that more fully answers all the needs of my mind and heart; if I find such a truth, I shall immediately accept it, for God requires nothing except truth. But I can no more return to the place from which I have just, with such suffering, emerged, than a flying bird can re-enter the shell from which it hatched.

'He who begins by loving Christianity better than truth, will proceed by loving his own sect or church better than Christianity, and end in loving himself (his own peace) better than all', said Coleridge.

I have gone the opposite way. I began by loving my Orthodox faith more than my own peace, then I loved Christianity more than my own church, and now I love truth more than anything else in the world. And to this day truth corresponds for me to Christianity as I understand it. And I hold to this Christianity; and in so far as I hold to it I live calmly and joyfully, and calmly and joyfully approach my death.

The Diaries
and The Letters

Since most of Tolstoy's religious writings were forbidden by the censor, he propagated his ideas not only by publishing his writings (in underground presses or abroad) but also by keeping a copious diary and writing long letters to anyone who was interested in his point of view. His diary by the late 1880s was not a secret thing (though he did keep a secret journal hidden in the toes of his boots!). It was left open on the table at Yasnaya Polyana and could be read by visitors and house guests. His later diaries contain some of his profoundest reflections, but he is best heard in his letters. Tolstoy was good at talking to people. When he was able to keep his temper, he was a good controversialist. The letters give us a vivid flavour of what it might have been like for us, if we had made the pilgrimage to Yasnaya Polyana and gone for a walk with the old man.

Tolstoy has a tremendous capacity to annoy people, and those who disagree with his religious opinions like to dismiss him as a humbug or a hypocrite. He has a good answer for them in the paragraph beginning on page 147, 'There is another question. . . .'

He was not an easy man to have as a husband, or as a father. His own childhood was, for him, too difficult to escape. In the lives of his children, he had a tendency to see a hideous re-enactment of his own youthful mistakes and follies. I have chosen to end this selection with a long letter which Tolstoy wrote to his son Mikhail – his youngest son to survive childhood. When he was sixteen, Mikhail went down into the village and got interested in one of the peasant girls, in exactly the same way as his father might have done at the same age. This is the letter he received. It sets out very plainly the secret of true happiness, as explained to the world by Jesus. But as we read it, every paragraph makes clear why – ever since that secret was expounded two thousand years ago in Galilee – the human race has been blocking its ears.

The Diaries

23 November 1888, Moscow

The other day a young girl came round, asking (such a common yet spurious question) what she could do in order to be of use. After talking to her for a while I understood: it was the same tragedy that afflicts millions of people – not so much that they live bad lives as that they do not live in accord with their conscience, with their own conscience. People follow some other conscience instead of their own, some higher conscience (Christ's is the most common example); and then, since they are clearly incapable of living in accord with this other conscience, they end up following no conscience at all, neither this other conscience nor their own. I tried to persuade this young lady to live in accord not with my conscience – as she wished – but with her own. But she, poor girl, did not know whether she possessed any conscience of her own. All this is a great evil. What people need most of all is to develop their own conscience, to clarify it to themselves and then live in accord with it; what they do instead is to choose some foreign, inaccessible conscience and then live quite without conscience, lying and lying in order to make it seem as though they are living in accord with this foreign conscience. Really I prefer some jovial, hard-drinking fellow, someone who keeps all reasoning at arm's length, to the philosopher who lives in accord with someone else's conscience, i.e. without any conscience at all. The former may yet develop a conscience, while the latter will never do so until he returns to the condition of the former.

1) The true enchantress is love. One need only love – and what one loves becomes splendid. But what must one do in order to love, in order to love everything? 'Not beloved because beautiful, but beautiful because beloved.' But what must one do? I know one thing: not to allow temptations to get in the way of love and, above all, to love love, to be aware that life lies only in love, that without it there is only suffering.

2) I remembered how often I used to argue with religious dogmatists, Orthodox, Evangelists and others. How absurd! How can one seriously argue with a man who claims that there is only one correct view of the world and our place in it, a view articulated by the council of bishops called 1500 years ago by Constantine in Nicaea and which states that God is the Trinity and that 1800 years ago He sent His son to a virgin in order to redeem the world, etc. One cannot argue with such people, one can nurse them, feel sorry for them, attempt to heal them, but one must look on them as spiritually sick and not argue with them.

3) Dissatisfaction with oneself is a sign of friction, a sign of movement.

4) There is not one believer who does not suffer moments of doubt in the existence of God. These doubts are not harmful; on the contrary, they lead to a higher understanding of God. The God you know is familiar and you no longer believe in Him. You believe fully in God only when He reveals Himself to you anew. And He reveals a new side of Himself only when you seek for Him with all your soul.

5) What I want to write now is very confused, but it brought me great joy and excitement when it first occurred to me.

If 'I' am 'I', the same 'I' as sixty or thirty years ago, or two hours ago, it is because I love this 'I'; because love binds these separate 'I's, these 'I's that are spread out over time into one whole. With regard to time I can clearly see how love binds together these different 'I's and gathers them into one. With regard to space the same thing happens in my body. A physiologist would say that my hand is my 'I' because I am one organism and my nerves inform me of this unity through pain. But why do I feel pain? Because I love everything that makes up my body. Love has knitted it together. Dickens writes of an amputee who carries his leg around in a bottle and loves it. A mother loves the locks of hair cut from her child, and feels pain when they are destroyed. In the same way one can love people who lived before, people who are ill, and their sufferings. Love for one's 'I' within certain limits of space and time is what we call life. This love for one's 'I' is a love that has crystallized and become unconscious, while love for other beings in space and time may perhaps be a preparation for another life. Our life is the fruit of the preceding sphere of love, while our future life will depend on the extent of our sphere of love in this life. How? There are many abodes. It hasn't worked out.

6) How astonishing it is that the infinity of space and time is often adduced as a proof of the power of human reason, whereas in reality there is no more obvious proof of the inadequacy, narrowness, shortsightedness, even falsity of human reason, than its inability to conceive of anything except in space and time. The concepts of space and time are absurd, quite contrary to the demands of reason. Space is supposed to show us the limits of the disposition of things, and time is supposed to show us the limits of the sequence of things, but in reality neither space nor time have any limits. I know of no more precise definition of time and space than the one I worked out for myself as a fifteen-year-old: time is man's ability to conceive of many objects in one and the same space – which is possible only through temporal sequence – while space is man's ability to conceive of many objects at one and the same moment of time – which can be done only by arranging them beside one another. Time and space can be defined as human abilities, but as properties of things themselves they are meaningless. It would be quite logical if I were to say that it is characteristic of me that everything I see, I see only in space and time; it would be absurd, however, if I were to imagine that things themselves really only exist in space and time, if I were then to become

absorbed both by questions about the origin of things, about the origin of the world, going further and further back in time ad infinitum, and by questions about where things are and what sort of things they are, about the worlds beyond this world and so on ad infinitum.

The Letters

If a woman flogs her child before my eyes, what should I do? Please understand that I am asking not what my first impulse would be, but what I ought to do, what would be most useful and sensible. If someone offends me personally my first impulse is to take revenge, but I am asking whether or not this is sensible. Whether or not one should use violence against a mother flogging her child is exactly the same question. If a mother flogs her child, what is it that upsets me, what is it that I see as evil? The fact that it hurts the child, or the fact that the mother is experiencing the torments of anger instead of the joys of love? I consider both of these to be evil. One person alone cannot commit evil. Evil is a disconnection between people. And so, if I act, I can only do so with the aim of destroying this disconnection, of restoring the connection between the mother and her child. How should I act? Should I use violence against the mother? That would do nothing to restore her connection with the child, and would only serve to introduce a new sin, a disconnection between her and me. What can be done then? There is one thing that would not be foolish, and that is to take the place of the child oneself. What Dostoevsky writes and I myself find abhorrent is something I have often heard from monks and metropolitans – that it is permissible to make war, since to lay down one's life for one's brothers is an act of defence; I have always answered that to expose oneself, to protect another with one's own chest, is one thing, but that to shoot someone with a rifle is very different indeed. Read the teachings of the gospels and you will see that the brief precept not to resist evil, not to repay evil for evil (Matthew 5:38–9), is the connecting link – if not the core – of the whole teaching; it is this precept that false Christian teachings have always carefully passed over; and it is a refusal to acknowledge this precept that serves as a foundation for everything that you so justifiably hate. There is no need to talk of the church of Nicon which brought about so much evil and was itself founded on this same misunderstanding of Christ's teaching, i.e. that it is right to commit acts of violence in the name of Good and Christ; even in the Acts of the Apostles one can see the destruction of the meaning of the teaching, the germs of this violence carried out in the name of Good.

How often I have felt amused while talking to priests and revolutionaries, both of whom look on the gospel teachings as a means of achieving an external goal; members of these two opposite camps deny the basis of Christ's teaching with equal fury. The priests find it impossible not to persecute, not to stifle dissent, not to give their blessing to executions and carnage; the revolutionaries cannot help but use violence in order to destroy the present appalling disorder, which is considered to be order. The priests and the powers-that-be are clearly unable even to imagine life without violence; and the revolutionaries are the same. By its fruits you shall know the tree; a good tree cannot bear fruits of violence. The teaching of Christ cannot be used to support either suppression or insurrection. By distorting the teaching, both sides deprive themselves of the unique power that springs from faith, not just in one part of the truth, but in the whole of it. Those who live by the sword shall die by the sword; this is not a prediction, but a statement of a fact known to everyone.

Matthew 6:22, 23, 24, especially 23. If your light is in fact darkness, if what you consider to be good is evil, then imagine the evil of your life and works. It is impossible to serve partly God and partly the Devil. The gospels are not such a stupid book as the priests make out. Not one statement is made idly; every tenet is linked to the whole of the teaching. The precept of non-resistance to evil, for example, runs through the whole of the gospels, and without it, in my opinion, their teaching falls apart. Not only is it stated many times so clearly and directly that it cannot be glossed over; not only is the entire account of Christ's life and work an illustration of this tenet; not only did Caiaphas, as a result of his failure to understand this truth, bring about the death of Christ in the name of the good of the people (as St John describes); but more than that, it is directly stated that resistance to evil is the most terrible and dangerous of all temptations,the temptation to which Christ's disciples succumbed and to which He almost succumbed Himself. And I think now that even if Christ and His disciples had never existed, I would have discovered this truth for myself; that is how clear and simple it now appears to me, and I am sure that it will appear the same to you. It is clear to me now that if I allow myself to commit the slightest act of violence in order to correct the greatest of evils, then a second person will do the same, followed by a third and a fourth – and these millions of minor acts of violence will together constitute the same terrible evil which now holds sway over us and oppresses us.

If you have done as I asked and read calmly until now, refraining from bringing forward proofs of your own views, then I hope you will agree with me that there exists strong evidence for an opinion contrary to yours; and I hope that you will be still more ready to agree with me when you read the short exposition and the translation of the four gospels which I am sending to you. As far as I can guess, your position at present is as follows: your reason tells you that I am right, but your heart rebels against this understanding of non-resistance to evil. What you are saying to yourself is this: something is not right, there is some mistake here, I must find it and point it out. It cannot be that Christ's teaching of love for one's brother can lead one to sit with one's arms folded, gazing calmly at the evil that is performed in the world. It is all very well for Tolstoy, you say, an old man coming to the end of his life, to chatter away and assure people that evil must be endured. It is all very well for him, he is satisfied and has enough to eat, he has everything he needs, and does not have much longer to live. All his vital passion has been expended, but I myself can sense without taking thought that it is not for nothing that I have been imbued with love for what is good and true, and with hatred for what is false and evil; I cannot but express this and dedicate my life to it, my every step must be a struggle against evil. I must and will struggle, using all the means which come to hand and which I understand. It is necessary to preach to the people, to bring about a reconciliation with the sectarians, to bring pressure to bear on the government, etc.

It is a good feeling that prompts these thoughts, and I love you for it; but it was the same feeling that led Peter to carry a knife and cut off the slave's ear. Imagine what would have happened if Jesus had not restrained them; there would have been a brawl, Jesus and His disciples would have been defeated, and then Jerusalem would have been conquered. They would have used violence, and violence would have been used against them. And what would have happened to the Christian teaching? There would have been no such thing and we would have had no support; we would have been in a worse position than the Aksakovs and the Solovyovs.

In order to express my thoughts more completely to you, I will tell you what I see as the importance of Christ, an importance that is not vague and metaphysical but clear and vital.

Everyone says that the meaning of Christianity lies in loving God and one's neighbour as one loves oneself. But what is God? What is love? What does it mean to love something incomprehensible like God? What is one's neighbour? What am I? For me these words have the following meaning: to love God means to love the truth; to love one's neighbour as oneself means to acknowledge the union of the essence of one's own life and soul with that of every other human life and with the eternal truth which is God. That is how it is for me. But I can clearly see that these words, which define nothing, can indeed be understood differently, and that the majority of people may not understand them in the way I have done. How can one love some God or other, whom each person understands in his own way and some do not even acknowledge at all, and love one's neighbour as oneself, when one is imbued with a love for oneself which never leaves one for a moment, and often with an equally persistent hatred for others? This is so clear and impracticable as to remain a mere phrase. My own opinion is that this precept is a metaphysical one, very important as such, but simply absurd when it is understood as a law, as a rule for everyday life. And it is, unfortunately, all too often understood in this way.

I say all this in order to make it clear that the significance of Christianity, as of any other faith, lies not in its metaphysical principles (humanity's metaphysical principles, those of Buddha, Confucius and Socrates, have always been the same and always will be), but in their application to life, in the vital conception of the welfare of each individual and of all humanity which can be reached through applying these principles to life, in the understanding of the possibility of their application and in the definition of the rules through which this is attained.

It is said in Deuteronomy that one should love God and one's neighbour as one loves oneself, but the applications of this principle are limited to circumcision, the Sabbath and the criminal law. The significance of Christianity lies in its indication of the possibility of fulfilling the law of love and the happiness that this affords. In the Sermon on the Mount Christ very clearly defined how it is both possible and necessary, for one's own happiness and that of others, to fulfil this law. In the Sermon on the Mount, without which everyone agrees there would be no Christian teaching, in which Christ addresses not sages but the rude and the illiterate, in this sermon that is framed by a preface that 'Whosoever shall break one of these least commandments . . .' and a conclusion that one must not speak but act, in this sermon where everything is stated, we are given five precepts as to how to fulfil the law. The Sermon on the Mount lays down the simplest, easiest, most understandable laws for the expression of love towards God, towards one's neighbour, and towards life itself; without acknowledging and fulfilling these laws one cannot even speak of Christianity. And though it may indeed be strange to say this after 1800 years, it fell to me to discover these laws as though they were something new. And it was only when I understood these laws that I understood the significance of Christ's teaching. These rules so astonishingly embrace the entire life of each individual and of humanity as a whole that man need only imagine their fulfilment, and the kingdom of truth will be realized. And if you then analyse these rules separately and apply them to yourself, you see that this vast and unimaginably blessed result is achieved through the fulfilment of the simplest and most natural of laws, laws that are not only easy but even pleasant to fulfil. You may wonder whether it is necessary to add anything to these laws in order to realize the kingdom of truth. It is not. You may wonder whether it is possible to deny any of these rules without violating the kingdom of truth. It is not. If I knew nothing of Christ's teaching except these five rules I would still be as much of a Christian as I am now: 1) Do not be angry; 2) Do not commit fornication; 3) Do not swear oaths; 4) Do not go to law; 5) Do not go to war. This for me is the essence of Christ's teaching.

This clear expression of Christ's teaching was hidden from people, and so humanity continually deviated from it towards two extremes. Some people, seeing Christ's teaching as a teaching about the salvation of the soul, for the sake of an eternal life that they understood only crudely, withdrew from the world, taking concern only over what they should do for themselves, over how they could best perfect themselves in solitude; all this would be amusing if it were not so pitiful. Enormous efforts were expended by these men – and there were many of them – on something both stupid and impossible, on doing good for oneself in solitude. Other people, not believing in a future life, lived only for others – the best of them, that is – but did not know or even wish to know what they needed for themselves; they did not know what good was, nor in whose name they wished it to others. I think that the one is impossible without the other. A man cannot do what is good for his own soul unless – unlike the ascetics – he acts together with others and on their behalf; and he cannot do what is good for others unless – unlike public figures who themselves have no faith – he knows what he needs for himself and in whose name he acts. I love the first category of people, but I hate their teaching with my whole soul; and I love the second category of people, I love them very much, but I hate their teaching as well. Truth lies only in the teaching which requires activities that both satisfy the needs of the soul and at the same time are of benefit to others. Such is the teaching of Christ. It is equally distant from religious quietism and its exclusive concern for one's own soul, and from the revolutionary fervour (the activities of governments and priests are also revolutionary) which wishes to benefit others without knowing what constitutes true and indubitable good. Christian life is such that it is impossible to do good to others without doing good to oneself, to one's rational soul, and equally impossible to do good to oneself without doing good to one's brothers. Christian life is equally distant from both quietism and fervour. Young people and people of your way of thinking tend to confuse the quietism of superstition with the true Christian teaching. They imagine that it is very easy and comfortable to refuse to resist evil, and that such a refusal would weaken Christianity and sap its strength. This is not true. You must understand that a Christian renounces violence not because he does not love the same things as you do, but because he can clearly see that, although violence is man's first response to the sight of evil, it will take him not nearer to his goal but further away from it; he can clearly see that violence is irrational, just as it is irrational for a man wishing to reach the water of a spring to batter on the earth that separates him from it. A man who renounces violence will not find life any easier – any more than he would find it easier to take a spade and dig than to batter on the earth with a stake. Life is easier for him only in so far as he clearly knows that, through spreading goodness and truth instead of resisting evil with violence, he is doing what he can – in Christ's words – to fulfil the will of the Father. Fire cannot be quenched by fire, nor can water be quelled by water; no more can evil be destroyed by evil. People have tried to do this, they have tried to do this since the world began – and this is what has brought us to our present position. It is time to abandon the old method and take up a new one, all the more so since it is a more rational method. If there is any progress, it is only thanks to those who have repaid good for evil. What if one millionth part of the efforts devoted by people to overcoming evil through violence were devoted instead to enduring evil, refusing to participate in it and continuing to shine with the light that has been given to each of us? If only as an experiment (nothing has been achieved through the old method) why not try a new method, all the more so since it is so clear, so obvious and so joyful? One particular example: think of Russia during the last twenty years. What true desire for good, what readiness for sacrifice, what efforts our young intelligentsia have expended in order to establish truth, in order to do good to people! And what has been achieved? Nothing! Worse than nothing. Tremendous spiritual powers have been exhausted. Stakes have been broken and the earth has been packed down more firmly than ever; it is now impossible even to dig. Instead of the terrible sacrifices incurred by youth, instead of shots, explosions and printing presses, what if these people were to believe instead in the teaching of Christ, if they were to consider that a Christian life is the only rational life? What if, instead of these terrible exertions, one, two, dozens or hundreds of people were simply to say when they were called up for military service: 'We cannot be murderers since we believe in the teaching of Christ which you profess. It is forbidden by His commandment.' They would say the same with regard to the swearing of oaths; they would say the same with regard to law courts; they would say the same with regard to the use of violence to defend property. What the result of all this would be I do not know, but I do know that it would bring about progress, and that this is the one and only path of fruitful activity; not to do what contradicts the teaching of Christ but to affirm it directly and openly – not in order to attain any external goal, but for one's own inner satisfaction, which lies in not doing evil unto others while one has the strength to do good to them.

This is my answer to your questions as to what we should strive for. We should strive to fulfil Christ's laws ourselves and to reveal to others the light and joy that comes from this. All this, by the way, is said much better in the gospels: Matthew 5:13–16. I foresee another objection. You will say that it is not clear how we can fulfil these laws or where they will lead us. What, according to these laws, should be one's attitude to property, to the government, to international relations?

Do not think that any of Christ's words are unclear. Everything is as clear as day. The parable of the coin explains how one should relate to governments. Money and property are nothing to do with Christianity. They come from Caesar and should be rendered unto Caesar. But your free soul comes from the God of truth, and so your actions and your rational soul should not be rendered to anyone except God. People can kill you, but they cannot force you to kill or do anything unChristian. As regards property: according to the gospels there is no property, and woe betide those who possess it. Whatever situation a Christian may be in, all he can do with regard to property is to refuse to participate in the violence carried out in the name of property, and to explain to others that property is a myth, that there is no such thing as property, but only a certain evil and habitual violence with regard to what we refer to as property.

No one who gives his coat to a man who demands his shirt can talk about property. Nor can he talk about international relations. All people are brothers. If savages have come to burn my children, then all I can do is to attempt to convince them that this will do them no good. This is all the more true since it is senseless for me to struggle against them. Either they will overpower me and burn still more of my children, or else I will overpower them, and my children will suffer terrible pains and die of some illness.

So this is my answer: the best we can do is to fulfil the teaching of Christ ourselves. In order to do this, we must be certain that it is true for all humanity and for each of us. Do you have this faith?

As for your article, I think it would be best to print it, although with some cuts. There are two other objections or questions that I imagine you will want to address to me. The first is that if you do indeed submit in this way to savages and to the policeman, if you give an evil person everything he wants to take from you, if you refuse to have anything to do with such State institutions as law courts, colleges and universities, if you do not claim your own property, then you will fall to the lowest step of the social ladder. You will be obliterated and trampled on, you will become a wandering beggar, and the light that is in you, seen by no one, will be wasted. It would be better to keep oneself at a certain level of freedom from need, and reserve for oneself the possibility of education and communication – through the press – with as large a circle of people as possible. This does indeed seem to be the case, but it only seems so. It seems so because we value the comforts of life, together with our education and all the imaginary joys it affords us; and because of all this we lie to ourselves. In actual fact, whatever step a man may be standing on, he will always be with other people and so be in a position to do good to them. And whether university professors are more important for Christianity than people who live in a doss-house is a question that no one can answer, although my own instinct and the example of Jesus incline me in favour of the beggars. Only beggars can spread the good tidings, that is, teach the rational life. I may be able to argue eloquently and sincerely, but no one will ever believe me if they see that I live in a palace, and that my family spend more in a day than a poor family spends on food in an entire year. As for education, it is time we stopped talking about it as a blessing. It is certainly able to damage ninety-nine people out of a hundred, but it can never add anything to anyone. You probably know about Syutayev. He is an illiterate peasant, but his influence on people, his influence on our intelligentsia, is greater than that of all the Russian writers from Treyakovsky to the present day taken together, Pushkin and Belinsky included. So it is wrong to imagine that one will lose anything. And whoever leaves his home, his father and mother, his brothers, his wife and his children, will find in this world a hundred times more houses and fathers, and also eternal life. For many of those who are first shall be last: Matthew 10:29.

There is another question that must arise almost against your will. 'What about you, Lev Nikolayevich, you preach very well, but do you carry out what you preach?' This is the most natural of questions and one that is always asked of me; it is usually asked victoriously, as though it were a way of stopping my mouth. 'You preach, but how do you live?' And I answer that I do not preach, that I am not able to preach, although I passionately wish to. I can preach only though my actions, and my actions are vile. What I say is not a sermon, only a rebuttal of a false understanding of the Christian teaching and an explanation of its true importance. Its import is not that one should use violence in order to refashion society; its import is that one should find the meaning of life in this world. And if you carry out the five precepts, you will find this meaning. If you wish to be a Christian then you should carry out these precepts, and if you do not wish to carry out these precepts then you should not talk about a Christianity without these precepts. 'But,' people say to me, 'if you believe that there can be no rational life without fulfilling the Christian teaching, and if you love this rational life, why then do you not carry out the precepts?' And I answer that I am guilty, and vile, and worthy of contempt for my failure to carry them out. At the same time, not in order to justify, but simply in order to explain my lack of consistency, I say: 'Look at my present life and then at my former life, and you will see that I do attempt to carry them out. It is true that I have not fulfilled one thousandth part of them, and I am ashamed of this, but I have failed to fulfil them not because I did not wish to, but because I was unable to. Teach me how to escape from the net of temptations that surrounds me, help me and I will fulfil them; even without help I wish and hope to fulfil them. Attack me, I do this myself, but attack *me* rather than the path I follow and which I point out to anyone who asks me where I think it lies. If I know the way home and am walking along it drunkenly, is it any less the right way because I am staggering from side to side! If it is not the right way, then show me another way; but if I stagger and lose the way, you must help me, you must keep me on the true path, just as I am ready to support you. Do not mislead me, do not be glad that I have got lost, do not shout out joyfully: "Look at him! He said he was going home, but there he is crawling into a bog!" No, do not gloat, but give me your help and support.

'For you are not devils in the swamp, but people like me who are seeking the way home. For I am alone and it cannot be that I wish to go into the swamp. Help me, my heart is breaking in despair that we have all lost our way; and when I struggle with all my might, instead of pitying me if I take a false step, you just push me further and cry out joyfully: "Look, he's with us here in the swamp."'

So this is my attitude to the teaching and its fulfilment. I try to fulfil it with all my might. I not only repent for each failure, but also beg for help in fulfilling it. And I joyfully greet anyone who, like me, is looking for the path; and I listen to him.

If you read what I am sending you, you will be able to understand this letter more easily.

Write to me. I am very glad to be in communication with you and I am waiting anxiously for your answer.

Letter to M. L. Tolstoy

16–19 October 1895, Yasnaya Polyana

I am writing to you, Misha, and not just saying in words what I have to say, because some impenetrable barrier has come between us, a wall which allows no possibility of communication. Because of this wall we grow more and more distant from one another, so distant that it is already difficult for us to understand one another. It is in order to knock down this wall, in order to communicate something of great importance, without which your life will become more and more difficult, that I am now writing this letter. Please read it attentively and think over its content. It deserves such attention because it is with tenderness in my heart and tears I can barely hold back that I write it, that I attempt to say all that I have recently thought and felt in the course of many sleepless nights. What I write now applies also to Andryusha and to all young people in your position, although I write with you only in mind, and turn to you with the love I feel for you alone. I am not turning to Andryusha because he has already gone too far along the path of destruction you are following yourself; I have less hope of his understanding me, of his understanding my words as I understand them and attending to their meaning. You and I are like two people walking in different directions who met and then parted; the further they walk, the greater the distance between them, until there comes a time when they can only hear one another with great difficulty. I hope that the distance between us is still such that you can hear my voice; Andryusha, however, is already so far away that it is unlikely he should hear me. But the further he has gone, the more important it is that he hears; and so I shout to him at the top of my voice and I do not despair of his hearing and turning back, or even just stopping. I have just written to him, but what I wrote concerned mainly the difficult situation he is now in. I am writing to you in the hope of being able to forestall such a situation.

All young people of your age, living in the same conditions, are in a very dangerous situation. The danger lies in the fact that at an age when habits are formed which, like folds on a sheet of paper, will remain for ever, you live your lives without the slightest moral or religious restraint, aware on the one hand of the irksomeness of the teaching which has been forced on you, and which you try in one way or another to escape, and on the other hand of the multifarious pleasures of the flesh which tempt you on all sides and which you have it in your power to enjoy. This situation appears to you quite natural and cannot possibly appear otherwise; you are not in the least to blame for this since you grew up in the same situation and all your comrades are in the same situation; nevertheless it is something quite extraordinary and appallingly dangerous. It is dangerous because if, when one's desires are new and especially powerful, one's aim in life is that of you young people, then what follows is inevitable. In order to obtain the enjoyment to which one is accustomed from the satisfaction of one's desires – whether for sweet food, riding, games, fine clothes or music – it is necessary to add more and more objects of desire since lust, once satisfied, can never be content a second or third time with the identical pleasure, but requires new and stronger pleasures. (There is even a mathematical law according to which the degree of pleasure increases in arithmetical progression, while the means for producing this pleasure increase in geometrical progression.)

This is how it always goes: first berries, gingerbread and simple toys; then sweets, flavoured drinks, bicycles and horses; then cold meats, cheese, alcohol and women. And since sexual lust is the strongest of all lusts, expressed variously through falling in love, caresses, masturbation and copulation, it never takes very long before we reach this stage. Lastly, when it is no longer possible to replace these pleasures with anything new and more potent, we reach the stage of the artificial exaggeration of pleasures through self-intoxication, through alcohol, tobacco and sensuous music.

This path is so common that it is followed, with very few exceptions, by all young people, both rich and poor. If they stop in time, they move on to real life, crippled to a greater or lesser degree; otherwise they are entirely destroyed – as hundreds of young people have been destroyed before my own eyes, and as Andryusha is now being destroyed. It is a danger that has threatened all young people, both rich and poor, but it is clearly a greater danger for the rich – like yourself – since they are in a position to satisfy their lusts more quickly, and so are quicker to grow bored with the first stages and reach the final stage of women, intoxication and sensuous music. The danger is also especially great at the present day, when the old rules and ideals of life have been destroyed for most of your brothers, and the new rules and ideals have not only not been acknowledged by public opinion but – more than that – are generally made out to be strange, absurd and even harmful.

As someone who is very easily carried away, I myself in my own youth followed this same gradual progression in the satisfying of my lusts but, like all my contemporaries, I had very definite rules and ideals. These rules were very stupid, aristo-cratic rules, but they did serve as a restraint. To me, for example, it would have been as unthinkable to do what you do – to drink vodka with peasants and drivers or to make an exhibition before other people of your passion for a peasant girl – as it would have been unthinkable to steal or to kill. According to these ideals I was obliged to continue a way of life led by my father and grandfather, i.e. to establish a prominent and respected place for myself in society; in order to do this I had to be as finely educated as they were and as apparently noble. These ideals now seem quite ludicrous, you probably think the same yourself, but they did serve to restrain me, to divert me from what would have prevented me from living up to them. There still are aristocratic families where these ideals are still alive, where they do still keep the young people in check. I think you know some yourself. These ideals are outmoded and must inevitably break down, the young people brought up according to them will undergo great disillusion and suffering, but it is still better to have been imbued with such ideals. These people will not perish in the prime of life, as you, who have no ideals, may perish.

Your situation – and there are many people like yourself – is a very frightening one: you recognize no rules or ideals and so are hurtling, as though on rails, down the steep slope of lust. Inevitably you end up in the swamp which remains always the same, and which it is almost impossible to escape from – the swamp of wine and women.

There is only one way of salvation from your situation: to stop, to come back to oneself, to look round, to find ideals for oneself – to find what one wants to be – and then realize these ideals.

What is terrible about your situation is that, if you are honest people who do not for any reason lie to yourselves, then you know that the old beliefs, which were taught to you at school as the law of God, are an absurdity in which no one believes. You also know that the aristocratic ideals – according to which one must be an exceptional man in order to govern the mob, better, more educated and more refined than anyone else – are outmoded and destroyed. You can see that everyone around you lives with no rules or ideals except that of living as gaily as possible. If you ever hear or see that there are some people who profess strange ideas, who go around barely dressed, who eat badly, who do not drink or smoke, then everything you see, hear or even read about them convinces you that they are merely eccentrics, and that there is no need for you to find out any more about them. And you take no interest in them. And so all the young people of our time, yourself and Andryusha included, have decided unequivocally that you can search everywhere for an answer to any problems that arise for you – except among 'the benighted'. They are eccentrics, and that is that. You see me as a writer who has written splendid descriptions of balls, of hunting and races, but who now keeps saying and writing something strange and uninteresting that does nothing to help ordinary young people like yourself decide how they should act. You and my other relatives are particularly harsh and obtuse in this respect. You are like someone standing too close to an object and so unable to see it, when all he needs do in order to grasp it is to reach out his hand.

I find this especially painful, and it is this division between us – between me and the whole young generation – a division that has been artificially constructed by the enemies of good, that I want to destroy through this letter. 'Tolstoyans, "the benighted", Posha, Chertkov, people interested in vegetarianism and religion, are just eccentrics, ragamuffins, people who carry their own chamber-pots. There's nothing more to be said. It's quite clear that all this is fantasy, something impractical and quite inapplicable to life, of interest only to eccentrics and certainly not of any use to straightforward young fellows like us, who do not want to be different in any way and who want to live like everyone else.' It is this view of what I profess, of the work to which I have dedicated – and will continue until my last day to dedicate – all my powers, that upsets me most of all.

I profess and teach what I teach not because I enjoy doing so but because I know that it is the only way to save people, especially people at the beginning of their lives like yourself, from the misfortunes you are certain to suffer, and to bring to you the true good that you yourselves wish for. What I profess and teach is practical, simple and easy, whereas the aims you set yourself are fantastic, complicated and difficult.

The essence of what I teach, of what has been taught not by me alone but by Christ Himself and all the best people of the entire world, is to point out to you the calamities of your life – into which you fall unawares like butterflies attracted to a flame – and the good that has been preordained for you which, with equal lack of awareness, you mercilessly trample on and destroy. You live without any definite direction to your life except that in which you are drawn – here today, there tomorrow – by your lusts; and that is no way to live. The teaching of Christ which I profess will give you a direction, indicating a path which it is easy and joyful to follow although any deviation from it is punished by suffering. This teaching will give you a direction by pointing out the aim and meaning of life. Without it it is impossible to live, since it is the only way to control one's lusts.

What we call ideals are nothing other than an indication of the aim and meaning of life. Even if a man has only the lowest of ideals, that of the acquisition of wealth, this will serve to restrain his lusts. The ideals of ambition and fame will also serve to restrain lust. But all these ideals can be destroyed, and so what we need is an ideal that cannot be destroyed. And what such an ideal gives us is the meaning of life revealed by Christianity.

This meaning lies in the fact that our life has no goal in itself that could satisfy us. Its goal is outside us and inaccessible to us, and so the meaning of our life lies in our fulfilling what it is ordained for.

In order for us to find out what it is ordained for, we have been given reason, a capacity which we all possess and which allows us both to share what has been discovered by the reason of people who lived thousands of years ago, and to communicate what our own reason discovers to people who live thousands or millions of years after us. Compliance with what has been discovered by reason is the meaning of life; it is the highest good that is accessible to us.

Compliance with what reason has discovered, far from being something indefinite and non-essential – as it may seem to those who have never thought about the significance of reason – is something very well defined indeed which immediately imposes clear and straightforward obligations on us. The demands of reason are not just the demands of your own personal reason as it considers the phenomena of the world, but the demands of the reason of all humanity, as expressed in the words, rules and teachings that have been transmitted to us. This does not mean that we must accept everything that has been passed on to us from the ancients; it means that we must use our own reason to weigh up what has been passed on to us. We must then accept what conforms with our own reason and make it into the guiding principle of our life.

For example, an ancient and supposedly rational teaching has been passed on to me that God consists of three persons, that Christ is God, and that one should receive communion, etc. My reason does not accept this, and so I do not instate these demands as a guiding principle. On the other hand, I have also been told of a number of rules: that I should not do unto others what I should not like them to do unto me; that all men are brothers; that since man cannot give life, he should not take life; that man should constantly aspire to perfection; that he should not fall into despair if he sins, but should simply reform and attempt not to sin again; that people need to love one another and forgive one another; that one should take pity on those who are suffering and offer them help; that it is necessary for the welfare of all that each man should love one woman as his wife, and each woman love one man; that it is necessary for the welfare, both of society as a whole and of each individual, that every man should work and not exploit the labours of others; that in order for everyone to be happy, each person should act in such a way that if others were to act likewise it would augment rather than decrease the happiness of all. These demands of reason – whether they are of ancient or modern origin, whether they are from China, India, Germany or France – conform with what I am told by my own reason, and I therefore accept them as the guiding principle of my life. This weighing up of the demands of ancient reason, this acceptance of what conforms with my own reason, is what I mean when I talk of following the demands of reason.

Since the world began, people have accumulated more and more of these instructions of reason. We now possess a set of very well-defined instructions, compliance with which will deliver us from suffering and bring us true happiness. It is these rational demands of the Christian teaching that I teach and profess; they are both clearly defined and obligatory.

The essence of the Christian teaching is that it reveals to man his true happiness, a happiness that lies in the fulfilment of his purpose. At the same time it points out any apparent joys and pleasures that may destroy this happiness. The Christian teaching refers to these false joys and pleasures as snares and temptations; it defines them in detail, cautions us against them, shows us ways of escaping from them, and promises us equally great joys and pleasures in exchange – as well as the true happiness intended for man.

The chief and fundamental temptation Christ's teaching warns us against is to believe that happiness lies in the satisfaction of one's personal lusts. The personality, the animal personality, will always seek for the satisfaction of its lusts; the temptation is to believe that such satisfaction will bring happiness. There is a vast difference between, on the one hand, feeling lustful desires, believing that their satisfaction will bring happiness and so intensifying them; and, on the other hand, knowing that such satisfaction will only remove one from true happiness and so moderating one's desires.

The nature of the temptation, if man only allows his reason to function, is clearly visible. As well as the fact that the satisfaction of any lust is realized at the expense of others and so only with struggle, every satisfaction of lust brings in its train the inevitability of new lusts that are more difficult to satisfy, and so on ad infinitum. In order to prevent reason from revealing the vanity of this temptation, yet another temptation arises, the most terrible temptation of all, that of stupefying one's reason through tobacco, alcohol and music.

All the minor temptations depend on these two principal temptations. It is these that snare and torment people, depriving them of their true happiness.

Man has been given the joy of food, the joy of appetite developed by labour and self-restraint. A crust of bread, if one is hungry, can be eaten with more pleasure than pineapples and truffles; and yet man arranges his life so that he is hardly ever hungry. He spoils his appetite with food that is over-spiced, fatty and artificial, and then receives no pleasure from it, suffering instead from indigestion and stomach pains.

Man has been given the pleasure of exercising his muscles in work and the joys of rest; and yet he makes other people work for him, depriving himself of these joys and losing both the skill and the ability to work.

Man has been given the happiness of associating with other people, of friendship and brotherhood; and yet, instead of enjoying this, he sets himself apart from everyone else through pride, and limits his dealings to a small circle of people who for the main part are worse than he is himself. Man has been given the enormous happiness of family love; and yet he squanders this happiness through masturbation or depravity.

Man has been given the supreme joy of knowing himself to be a rational being; and yet he withdraws from the activities prescribed by his reason, stifling it through tobacco, alcohol and other vanities, and lowering himself to the level of an unreasoning animal.

This is the teaching I hold and profess, the teaching you and many others believe to be nebulous, fantastic, strange and impractical. Its essence is simply not to act vainly or stupidly, without profit either to yourself or to others; not to destroy the divine power that lies within one; and not to deprive oneself of the happiness intended for one. The essence of the teaching is to trust one's reason, to guard it in all its purity, to develop it and so obtain the true, eternal happiness of true life, together with joys more intense than those that tempt you.

You wish for the joys of eating, and imagine that eating will grow more and more enjoyable; but your taste-buds grow blunt and you are soon deprived of the very finest of these pleasures.

You wish for the pleasures of peace and rest and you stop doing either physical or mental work; and so you lose the skill and ability to work and can no longer recognize the true joy of rest after labour.

You wish to distinguish yourself from others, to stand out from them in such a way as to attract the attention of people; but, instead of attention, you attract only envy and are deprived of the brotherly love that could have arisen between you.

You wish for the joys of sexual love; and you destroy the possibility of this love when the right time for it arises.

Man is a union of two principles: a physical, animal principle, and a rational, spiritual principle. The vital impulse, that both propels its own life and continues this life in distant generations, lies in the animal being; the rational, spiritual being directs this impulse. In the absence of reason life follows a predetermined direction, as in a plant or animal; but as soon as reason appears, then its role is to control life, to form and develop another higher, spiritual life. For reason not to be in control of the animal life – as is the case with people who fall into temptation – is an infringement of the correct development of animal life.

It goes without saying that the errors of certain people cannot disturb the general flow of life, that even these errors are necessary and fruitful in the general economy of life; nevertheless, these errors are disastrous for those who fall into them. Such people are like seeds from a tree that fail to germinate.

Only two paths are possible for a rational being bound to an animal life: the path of compliance with reason, of subordinating one's animal nature to reason, a path that is joyful, offering an awareness of eternal life and its joys; and the path of subordinating reason to one's animal nature, of exploiting it in order to gain animal ends, a path that leads to disaster, that deprives man not only of the awareness of eternal life, but even of the joys characteristic of an animal.

I have written all this in order that you should stop and

think; in order that you should realize that if you see no other meaning in life than the satisfaction of lust, then this is not because that is truly the case, but simply because you are in error; in order that you should realize that near you, close at hand, are instructions with regard to the errors into which you are drifting, and that you need only come to your senses in order to see this.

I write, above all, because it is desperately, desperately painful for me to see how you and many others are perishing, perishing terribly and in vain, while salvation is so easy and lies so close at hand.